contents

introduction

Flowers bloom in a blaze of seasonal colour and then fade, but trees and shrubs provide the focal point and form the framework of the well-planned garden. Long-lived and easy to care for, trees and shrubs come in an amazing variety of shapes and sizes. There are dwarfs for the tiny town garden, tall, slender fastigiates for the narrow plot, magnificent broad-leaved, full-headed forms for the large garden. Climbing, flowering, creeping, fruit-bearing, fragrant, weeping.

And trees and shrubs provide season-spanning interest. Many have striking foliage; others have beautiful and unusual bark. Some are most effective as a background foil for the other plants in the garden, while some provide shelter and dappled shade to protect less hardy flora. Chosen carefully, trees and shrubs provide interest and contrast throughout the year with a minimum of care and attention.

TREES AND SHRUBS is the gardener's guide to deciduous and evergreen plants, complete with detailed information for planning your garden, large or small, to incorporate trees and shrubs into the overall scheme most effectively.

TREES

The Silver Birch (Betula pendula) is among the most graceful of native trees, well-known for its white bark, slender growth and delicate small leaves.

trees in the garden

Trees are the most long-lived growing features in any garden. Once they are well established, it is very difficult to move them; pruning them if they become too big is difficult, needing skilled workmanship, and is never a permanent solution to the problems of excessive roots and over-extensive shading that arise.

Since Victorian times the gardener's problems in tree-planting have been made much easier by the introduction of moderate sized trees from western China in particular, as well as Japan, and also by hybridisation and selection. These include excellent maples, white-beams, rowans, cherries and ornamental apples (crabs), as well as birches. Many of these also provide what is wanted in a small area, a tree that has more than one season of interest, such as decorative bark in mid-winter, attractive unfolding foliage in spring followed by a period of flowering, then brightly coloured fruit and finally gay colouring of the leaves before they fall. Trees often have at least two if not three seasons of interest.

Evergreen broad-leaved trees are of particular interest in winter, and many have variegated or coloured-leaved forms. All are least satisfactory in towns where air pollution takes away the shine of their foliage.

The same applies to conifers, a number of which are of too great a size and too fast-growing for gardens, and are seen at their best in forests.

For road planting and use in smaller gardens narrow (fastigiate) forms of many trees have been selected and are propagated as cultivars. They are also useful in planting on a large scale on account of their beautiful shape. This applies also to the numerous weeping trees available.

Soil

Hardy trees are surprisingly tolerant of soil conditions provided drainage is good. Many come from mountains where soil is not deep, except in the river valleys.

Where the soil is well drained, the limiting factor for a number of species is the amount of lime present. Many trees growing naturally on acid or neutral soils will grow equally well on soils with a moderate lime content, particularly if the soil is deep and fertile. But a certain number are, like rhododendrons among shrubs, strongly lime-hating plants, particularly on rather shallow, chalky soils.

Apart from the degree of soil alkalinity, depth and soil structure affect the kind of trees that can be grown. In general, with certain notable exceptions, conifers prefer acid or neutral soils. The *Rosaceae*,

however, has many genera that are often associated in nature with alkaline soils such as *Malus* (apples), *Prunus* (cherries, plums, peaches, almonds, etc.), *Pyrus* (pears), *Crataegus* (thorns) and *Sorbus* (rowans and service trees).

It is curious that though many acid-loving plants will not live in limy soils most of those that are lime-loving will grow well in neutral and acid soils.

The following list indicates the preferences of some commonly cultivated genera, particularly those that will, or will not, grow on soils with a moderate lime content, and those that will on no account tolerate shallow, chalk soils.

Broad-leaved trees

ACER Most maples thrive on lime and chalk, including British natives and those commonly planted. The Chinese species, such as *A. capillipes, davidii, ginnala, griseum* and *rufinerve*, make a splendid display in chalk gardens. *A. palmatum* and its cultivars need more fertile soil. The American *A. rubrum* will not grow on chalk.

1 Liriodendron tulipifera, the tulip tree, will grow on limy soil.
2 Ulmus stricta, the Cornish elm, grows well on chalk.
3 Acer pseudoplatanus 'Leopoldii' has silvery-yellow leaves.

AILANTHUS Tolerates lime.

ALNUS All alders will grow well on lime but must have moisture, with the exception of *A. cordata* and *A. incana*, which will stand drier situations. The former is good on chalk.

AESCULUS The horse-chestnuts and buck-eyes do well on lime and chalk, though preferring fertile soils.

AMELANCHIER Though naturally growing on light acid soils, these will tolerate some lime.

ARBUTUS One of the few *Ericaceae* that grows well on lime.

BETULA The birches do well on lime.

BUXUS Good on lime, the common box grows naturally on chalk.

CARPINUS All the hornbeams are successful on either heavy alkaline soils or light chalk.

CARYA Will tolerate some lime in deep fertile soils.

CASTANEA The sweet chestnuts do not like lime, but will tolerate it in small quantities on well-drained fertile soils.

CATALPA Lime tolerant.

CERCIDIPHYLLUM Lime tolerant.

CERCIS The Judas trees do well on lime and chalk.

CORYLUS Hazels do well on lime, including chalk.

COTONEASTER Most kinds do well on lime, including chalk.

CRATAEGUS All thorns will grow on lime and chalk.

DAVIDIA The dove tree does well on lime and chalk.

EUCALYPTUS There is still some doubt as to which species will grow well on lime.

EUONYMUS The tree-like species thrive on lime and chalk.

FAGUS The beeches have a shallow root system and thrive on well-drained soils with high lime content and on chalk.

FRAXINUS The ashes thrive on soils with high lime content as long as they are fertile.

HALESIA The snowdrop trees will not tolerate lime.

ILEX Hollies are good on lime and chalk.

JUGLANS Walnuts will thrive on lime soils and chalk if it is not too thin.

KOELREUTERIA The golden rain tree will grow in any well-drained soil.

LABURNUM Will grow anywhere.

LIQUIDAMBAR Dislikes more than a trace of lime and will not grow on chalk.

LIRIODENDRON The tulip trees will grow on fertile soils with high lime content but are not happy on chalk.

MAGNOLIA Magnolias are not happy on limy soils, the exceptions among the tree-sized species being *MM. delavayi, X highdownensis, kobus, sinensis* and *wilsonii*.

MALUS In varying degrees the ornamental species and hybrids of apples are satisfactory on lime, and the majority do well on chalk.

NOTHOFAGUS The southern beeches so far in cultivation in temperate climates will, on fertile soils, stand a little lime in the soil but cannot be grown on chalk.

NYSSA A lime hater.

PARROTIA Is not successful where there is more than a trace of lime.

PAULOWNIA Good on lime and chalk.

PLATANUS The planes do well on lime.

POPULUS Poplars in general need fertile moist soil and will not object if there is a lime content, but, except for *PP. alba, canescens* and *lasiocarpa*, they will not grow on chalk.

PRUNUS Almonds, apricots, bird cherries, cherries (including the Japanese cultivars), laurels (common cherry and Portugal) and peaches, all grow on soils with a lime content and, in varying degrees, are also successful on chalk.

PYRUS The pears will all grow on soil with a high lime content, including chalk.

QUERCUS Most oaks do well on soils with a high lime content, including chalk, if there is sufficient depth for their tap-roots. Particularly good are *QQ. canariensis, cerris, frainetto, hispanica* 'Lucombeana', *ilex, macranthera, robur* and *petraea*. Willow oaks, *Q. phellos*, and cork oaks, *Q. suber*, are not good on lime.

RHUS The tree-like species will grow on lime, including chalk.

ROBINIA The false acacias will grow on lime soils and chalk, but are not at their best on them.

SALIX The tree-sized willows tolerate lime, but all need abundant moisture, and will not thrive on dry, chalk soils.

SAMBUCUS The common elder will reach tree size on lime and chalk.

SOPHORA Tolerates lime on well-drained fertile soils.

SORBUS The rowans and service trees are all good on lime, including chalk.

TILIA The commonly cultivated lime trees grow naturally on limestone formations, but need moderately fertile soils.

ULMUS All elms will grow well on lime and in varying degrees on chalk.

ZELKOVA The ironwoods will tolerate lime but must have deep fertile soils.

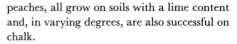

1 X Cupressocyparis leylandii, the Leyland cypress, grows on lime or chalk.
2 Tsuga mertensiana, the mountain hemlock, dislikes chalk and lime.
3 Araucaria araucana, the monkey puzzle, has an unusual appearance.

1 2 3

Coniferous trees

ABIES Most silver firs need deep, moist soil and in such will tolerate lime. *AA. amabilis, bracteata, forrestii, grandis, mangifica, procera* and *veitchii* are not good on soils with much lime. *AA. cephalonica* and *pinsapo*, however, will grow on chalk.

ARAUCARIA The monkey puzzle given fertile soil will tolerate lime and chalk.

CEDRUS All the cedars, especially *C. atlantica*, will tolerate lime on fertile soils.

CHAMAECYPARIS CC. lawsoniana and *nootkatensis* and their cultivars do well on soils with high lime content. *CC. obtusa, pisifera* and *thyoides* are not good on lime and will not thrive on shallow chalk.

CRYPTOMERIA The Japanese cedar will tolerate lime if grown in deep, moist soil.

X CUPRESSOCYPARIS The Leyland cypress grows well on lime and chalk.

CUPRESSUS The hardy cypresses will tolerate lime, and *C. macrocarpa* does well on chalk.

GINKGO The maidenhair tree grows well on fertile soils containing lime.

JUNIPERUS The numerous species and their cultivars grow well on lime.

LARIX Larches grow well on lime.

LIBOCEDRUS The incense cedar needs deep moist loam and will tolerate some lime.

METASEQUOIA The dawn redwood does best on fertile soils, with or without some lime, and will grow slowly and healthily on chalk.

PICEA The spruces are not happy on shallow, dry soils, though most will tolerate some lime, including the much cultivated common spruce, *P. abies*. An exception is the striking Serbian spruce, *P. omorika*, which grows on limestone rocks.

PINUS Though many of the pines grow naturally on light, mountain soils and many will tolerate a little lime, the majority dislike it. Even the Scots pine, *P. sylvestris*, is not at its best on lime. *PP. armandii, contorta, pinaster, radiata,* and *strobus* are unsatisfactory on lime. The handsome stone pine, *P. pinea*, will stand a little. The Austrian pine, *P. nigra austriaca* is good on chalk, as to a slightly lesser extent is the Corsican pine, *P. nigra maritima. P. mugo*, often no more than a spreading shrub, will also grow on chalk, as will the rare *P. bungeana*.

PSEUDOTSUGA The Douglas firs thrive on fertile, moist, well-drained soils, on which they will stand some lime but not chalk.

SEQUOIA The giant redwood will tolerate lime if there is a good depth of fertile soil but will not grow on chalk.

SEQUOIADENDRON The wellingtonia also will grow well in deep fertile soils but will not grow on chalk.

TAXODIUM The swamp cypress will not tolerate lime.

TAXUS The yews grow naturally on limestone formations and chalk, and are equally good on acid soils.

THUJA The western red cedar will grow on soils containing lime, as will the Chinese and American arbor-vitae and their cultivars.

TSUGA The western hemlock will not thrive on shallow soils containing lime or on chalk, nor will the other species occasionally planted. The eastern hemlock, *T. canadensis*, will, however, grow under these conditions.

Moisture content

The other soil factor that must be taken into consideration is continuous moisture, that is, soils that are continuously saturated. The majority of trees will not grow in these conditions but those that will include the numerous kinds of willow (*Salix*), large and small, as well as the alders (*Alnus*), which are mostly trees of moderate size. The handsome and uncommon swamp cypress, *Taxodium distichum*, is also good, though very wet conditions are not necessary for its success.

Planting

A tree will normally outlive its planter. However, if it is given a good start the planter will be rewarded all the earlier by vigorous growth. Do not attempt to plant a tree in unsuitable soil. The choice having been made, you should assure yourself that you are buying stock of good quality.

Broad-leaved trees (deciduous or evergreen)

These may be purchased as standards, in which the clear stem is from about $5\frac{1}{2}$ to 7ft (1.68 to 2.13m). The smaller size is more satisfactory as a rule, and will soon catch up a larger one, which may well have an undesirably spindly stem. In some instances, when, as in a Japanese cherry, low branching will look attractive, a half-standard can be used branching at from $3\frac{1}{2}$ to $4\frac{1}{2}$ft (1.07 to 1.37m).

Have ready a sound, pointed stake long enough when driven firmly into the ground to reach to the point on the stem where the branching starts. You also need one of the several types of tree ties now available.

Dig or fork around where the tree is to be planted for about an area of a yard square (one metre square). Particularly if the ground is poor or heavy, work in some well-rotted compost or peat.

Remove the wrappings of the roots and cut off any that are broken. Dig a hole which will take the root system, as nearly as possible so that when the tree is stood in it, the soil mark on the stem is level with, or just below, the surrounding soil. It is, except where willows are concerned, very bad practice to plant too deeply. When you have ensured that the planting hole has been dug to the correct depth, lift the tree out and drive the stake well in at about the centre of the hole.

Replace the tree, working the roots round the stake so that the stake is as close as possible to the stem. This is easily done if someone else holds the tree in place. If you are working single-handed, loosely tie the tree to the stake.

Work soil carefully among the roots, gently shaking the tree up and down to settle the fine soil among the fine roots. Then almost fill the hole, frequently firming it by gentle treading. Next water the tree well; when the water has sunk in, lightly fill the hole up. Finally, attach the tie at the top of the stem.

Conifers

Conifers supplied are usually of a much shorter length than broad-leaved trees and seldom need staking. It is most important to disturb the root ball as little as possible. The sacking (burlap) which binds the ball may be left on until the tree is in the hole. The knot or lacing that holds it is then cut and gently teased loose and left in the hole. If the tree is not absolutely firm, a stout garden cane and strong string should be sufficient to secure it.

Planting of deciduous trees should be done as soon after leaf fall as possible, but may continue until early spring before the buds begin to break.

Conifers are best planted in autumn, when they will make root at once, and be established by spring. It is less desirable to plant in winter when the roots are for long quite inactive. Early spring is the next best time, for root growth will soon be active. But watering during a spring drought with an east wind is then essential. A mulch is also helpful.

Maintenance and pruning

The area round the base of the tree should be kept weeded until it is well established. Watch the tie regularly and keep it from becoming too tight, that is allow a little play. Strangulation may cause great damage. Remove the stake only when the tree is absolutely firm – this will take at least three years.

To keep the tree shapely, preferably with a single leading shoot, the following rules should always be followed in pruning trees young or old.

Always cut a shoot or branch back to the point where it arises, making the cut as clean and flush and as close to the main branch as possible. If a snag is left, it may die and eventually rot and cause damage.

If the shoot or branch is of any weight, carry out the operation in two stages, the first taking off the weight and leaving a short snag that can then be removed without its bark tearing away back into the main stem. If the scar is large, paint it with one of the proprietary sealing paints.

Ornamental trees are in general best pruned from mid-to-late summer. The wounds then heal quickly and attacks by fungi or bacteria are held at bay. This applies particularly to most species of *Prunus*, especially cherries. It also applies to maples, birches and walnuts which 'bleed' sap during the winter and spring.

Never attempt to carry out pruning on a large tree; always obtain the services of a qualified tree surgeon. Unless properly done, it will probably result in damage and disfigurement of the tree, and in addition is often a highly dangerous undertaking for the unskilled operator.

A selection of garden trees

Decorative bark and foliage
Broad-leaved

ACER CAPILLIPES Young bark striated with white; young growths coral red, leaves turning crimson in autumn. *A. davidii*, young bark shiny green, striated with white; leaves usually turn yellow and purple in autumn. Long chains of winged seeds or keys striking. *A. griseum*, paper bark maple, the outer bark peeling in papery flakes to show the copper-coloured inner bark; opening leaves bronze coloured, turning red or orange in autumn. *A. grosseri*, *A. g. hersii*, young bark green or yellowish striated with white, leaves orange and crimson in autumn. *A. pensylvanicum*, moosewood, young bark green striped and patterned with white, the large leaves pinkish on opening turning clear in autumn. *A. rufinerve*, bark green, with an elaborate pattern of greyish markings, persisting on old trunks; leaves red when young and usually crimson in autumn.

BETULA PAPYRIFERA Paper-bark birch, shining white bark, the large leaves turning pale gold early autumn, making it more effective than other birches with coloured stems.

LIQUIDAMBAR STYRACIFLUA The American sweet gum has interesting corky bark in winter, the leaves usually turning crimson in autumn.

PARROTIA PERSICA Particularly good if trained to standard form, the grey bark flaking away in a pattern resembling the London plane, while the leaves turn brilliant golds and crimsons (see also Early flowering trees).

SORBUS AUCUPARIA BEISSNERI This handsome cultivar of the mountain ash has red branchlets and a copper-coloured trunk, the large leaves with deeply cut leaflets turning old gold in autumn.

Conifers

Many conifers with yellow, silver or variegated foliage (listed under those headings) give interest of form and foliage colour at all seasons. Some pines, when their lower branches are removed, also have interesting bark. *Pinus bungeana*, the lacebark pine, has bark which peels off in white patches; *P. nigra maritima*, the Corsican pine, develops a striking erect trunk with pale scales between fissures in the dark bark. The Scots pine, *P. sylvestris*, with its smooth pink or red bark in the upper part of the tree, is singularly picturesque. The bark of the well-named redwood, *Sequoia sempervirens*, never loses its astonishing colour. Except *P. bungeana*, which is rare and slow-growing, these trees are only suitable for large gardens or parks.

1 *The paper-thin bark of Betula ermanii is cream-coloured, and its branches are orange-brown.*

2 *Quercus ruber, the cork oak, has distinctive and unusual thick-ridged bark.*

3 and 4 *The shining purple-red bark of Prunus serrula, which looks like polished mahogany, peels away from the trunk in thin layers.*

Decorative winter bark

The principal decorative distinction of the following is their bark, the colouring of their foliage not being exceptional.

ARBUTUS X ARACHNOIDES Hybrid strawberry tree. Trunk and branches cinnamon red.

BETULA Several birches have singularly beautifully coloured bark, though this does not always show on young trees. Among the best are *B. albo-sinensis septentrionalis*, orange-brown with a grey bloom; *B. ermanii*, trunk cream-coloured, the bark peeling off, the branches orange-brown; *B. jacquemontiana*, the whitest bark of all – the white can be rubbed off like chalk; *B. lutea*, the peeling, paper-like bark being yellowish; *B. pendula*, the European birch, varies greatly in the colour of its stem and good white-barked seedlings must be selected.

CORNUS MAS Old trees of cornelian cherry have trunks with attractive shaggy bark.

EUCALYPTUS Several species have interesting grey, peeling bark.

PLATANUS X HISPANICA The peeling of patches of bark showing the greenish grey inner bark of the London plane is well known.

POPULUS ALBA The bark of the white poplar is smooth and grey, with black markings, except at the base of the trunk; *P. canescens*, the grey poplar, has bark of a distinctive yellowish-grey colour.

PRUNUS MAACKII The Manchurian bird cherry has smooth bark, brownish-yellow in colour, and peeling like that of a birch; *P. serrula*, the bark is shiny, mahogany coloured, from which the thin outer skin peels, the trunk of a mature tree having narrow white scars around it.

QUERCUS SUBER The thick, ridged bark of the cork oak, not hardy in cold situations, makes it a distinctive tree.

SALIX DAPHNOIDES The violet willow owes its name to the purple shoots covered with a bloom giving them in places a violet colour; *S. purpurea*, the purple osier, has reddish-purple slender branches.

Beautiful flowers

AESCULUS CARNEA The red hybrid horse chestnut is very variable, the cultivar 'Briotii' should always be chosen. *A. hippocastanum*, the common horse-chestnut, growing into a very large tree, is well known. The double-flowered 'Baumannii' is smaller and does not produce conkers. *A. indica*, the Indian horse-chestnut, has the largest flower spikes of all, pink-flushed, in summer; *A. octandra*, the sweet buckeye, a smaller tree, has flowers that are pale yellow; *A. pavia* var. *atrosanguinea* is a small tree with crimson flowers in early summer.

CATALPA BIGNONIOIDES The Indian bean has many foxglove-like flowers in a pyramidal, erect spike in summer. The individual flowers are white marked with yellow and purple. Does well in the heart of a city.

CRATAEGUS The many-flowered inflorescences of the numerous thorns, mostly with white but sometimes red or pink flowers, are well known and very similar. A choice should be made from those that also bear showy fruits.

DAVIDIA INVOLUCRATA The pocket-handkerchief, or dove, tree has its small flowers surrounded by two large white bracts, making it a remarkable sight in spring.

FRAXINUS ORNUS In spring the manna or flowering ash is usually densely covered with clusters of small, creamy-white flowers.

KOELREUTERIA PANICULATA The golden-rain tree or pride of India carries in late summer erect pyramidal spikes of many small yellow flowers each with a red spot at the centre. The foliage also is attractive.

LABURNUM By far the best, with the longest chains of flowers and the sweetest scent, is the hybrid *L. X watereri* 'Vossii'.

MAGNOLIA Of the large tree magnolias, the following have large and magnificent flowers; *M. campbellii* (pink), *M. delavayi* (creamy-

1 Laburnum X vossii is one of the best of the sweet-smelling laburnums.
2 The leaves of Ailanthus altissima, the tree of heaven, and are long and attractive.
3 Aesculus X carnea, the red hybrid horse chestnut, is quite variable.

white), *M. denudata* (pure white), *M. grandiflora* (white), *M. mollicomata* (rose-purple), *M. obovata* (creamy-white), *M. sargentiana* (rose-pink), *M. tripetala*, umbrella tree (cream-coloured).

MALUS There are very many floriferous crab-apples, both with white, pink and red coloured flowers. It is best to choose those which also produce interesting fruit or have coloured foliage.

PAULOWNIA *P. fargesii* and *P. tomentosa* (syn. *P. imperialis*) have broad spikes of heliotrope foxglove-shaped flowers up to 1ft (305mm) long which are not produced every year, because of winter frost damage to the flower buds.

PRUNUS A selection from this very floriferous genus is best made when a second attribute, such as early flowering, decorative fruit, autumnal leaf colour or decorative bark is present. The Japanese cherries, with flowers ranging from white to shades of pink and even yellow, must be chosen on beauty of flower alone.

SORBUS The rowans and service trees have decorative clusters, in some kinds large, of white or rarely pink flowers, but they are best selected by giving attention to the merits of their foliage and berries.

TILIA The very many small clusters of pale yellow flowers that are carried by all species of limes in mid-summer must be mentioned if

only on account of their scent. *T. cordata* is the best for a small space, as it is slow growing.

Exceptionally handsome foliage – deciduous

AILANTHUS ALTISSIMA The tree of heaven has pinnate leaves sometimes 2ft (610mm) long.

CATALPA The Indian bean-trees have heart-shaped leaves up to 10in (254mm) long.

JUGLANS SIEBOLDIANA The walnuts all have handsome pinnate foliage, but in this species the leaves may reach 3ft (910mm) long.

MAGNOLIA DELAVAYI This evergreen tree has exceptionally handsome leaves 1ft (305mm) or more long. *M. tripetala*, the umbrella tree (so called because of the arrangement of its foliage) has very large leaves up to 20in (508mm) long.

POPULUS LASIOCARPA This has typical poplar-shaped leaves up to 1ft (305mm) long.

RHUS TYPHINA The pinnate leaves on the

stag's horn sumach may reach 3ft (910mm) long.

SORBUS HARROWIANA This tender species has the largest leaves of any mountain ash, 1ft (305mm) or more long. *S. sargentiana*, is a mountain ash which has leaves up to 1ft (305mm) long.

Autumn leaf display

It should be noted that autumn colour may vary from year to year in every respect, and even from tree to tree of the same species. This list is by no means complete.

ACER CAMPESTRE The European field maple turns a good yellow; *A. capillipes*, deep crimson; *A. cappadocicum*, yellow; *A. circinatum*, orange and crimson; *A. davidii*, variable, yellow and purple; *A. ginnala*, brilliant flaming scarlet; *A. griseum*, orange, bronze and fiery red; *A. grosseri*, also *A. g. hersii*, red and gold; *A. japonicum*, crimson and pink; *A. negundo*, clear yellow, early; *A. nikoense*, orange and red; *A. pensylvanicum*, clear yellow; *A. platanoides*, clear yellow; *A. rubrum*, scarlet and yellow; *A. rufinerve*, crimson.

AMELANCHIER All cultivated species turn shades of red and yellow.

BETULA Most birches turn shades of greenish yellow, but *B. papyrifera* is a good bright yellow.

CARYA Species usually cultivated turn a good yellow.

CERCIDIPHYLLUM JAPONICUM Variable, but can be brilliant in yellow and reds.

EUONYMUS SACHALINENSIS Yellow and red, early, with crimson fruits.

FAGUS The copper colour of the British native beechwoods is glorious in autumn.

FRAXINUS Most ashes turn shades of yellow before their leaves fall early in the season. *F. oxycarpa* 'Raywood', however, turns a distinctive purple.

GINKGO BILOBA The maidenhair tree turns a rich yellow.

LIQUIDAMBAR STYRACIFLUA Variable, but in good specimens can be brilliant, purple to scarlet.

LIRIODENDRON TULIPIFERA Leaves turn a good yellow.

MALUS Apples give little autumn leaf colour, an exception being *M. tschonoskii*, on which the leaves turn yellow and scarlet.

NYSSA SYLVATICA The tupelo turns vivid scarlet.

PARROTIA PERSICA Colouring unreliable, yellow through gold to crimson.

PRUNUS This genus provides only a few species that colour well, though the Japanese cultivars mostly turn good shades of yellow; *P. avium*, the gean, most years turns a flaming red; *P. sargentii*, infallibly turns a brilliant red early in autumn.

QUERCUS BOREALIS The red oak is rather a misnomer as the colour is nearer to brown, but it can be effective. *Q. coccinea*, the well-named scarlet oak, retains its brilliant leaves far into the winter, the best form being the cultivar 'Splendens'.

RHUS TYPHINA Turns orange, red and purple.

SORBUS CASHMERIANA Pale gold, falling early. *S. discolor*, brilliant red; *S.* 'Joseph Rock', leaves turn a rich variety of colours; *S. sargentiana*, striking reds and golds.

Autumn berry display

The following list is of trees whose brightly-coloured fruits are usually decorative for some time after the leaves have fallen. Birds soon attack and strip the berries on a number of kinds almost as soon as they are ripe, but the following are less severely attacked. With some trees, berries are only borne on female trees; in many instances nurserymen can select these.

CERCIS SILIQUASTRUM The Judas tree carries red-brown and purple pods from late summer far into the winter.

COTONEASTER FRIGIDUS Heavy crops of

1

2

3

clusters of rich bright red berries are borne in autumn and early winter.

CRATAEGUS All the thorns carry crops of haws, the more striking including *C. X lavallei* which has large orange-red berries that hang well into winter; *C. mollis*, the red haw, has very large red fruits which drop rather early to make a spectacular carpet under the tree; *C. orientalis* has large oval or yellowish-red fruits; *C. prunifolia* has large, red fruits, combined with crimson autumn foliage.

ILEX X ALTACLARENSIS I. aquifolium, the hollies, are among Britain's most beautiful berrying trees, though fruiting only on female trees. *I. a.* 'Bacciflava' ('Fructu-luteo') has yellow berries.

MALUS The crab-apples, mostly carry fruit. The best include the following: *M. X aldenhamensis*, fruit numerous small, deep purple; *M. eleyi*, bright crimson; *M.* 'Golden Hornet', bright yellow fruit – hanging late; *M.* 'John Downie', large, narrow fruits, yellow with red flush, flavour good.

PRUNUS though some of this genus, e.g., cherries, carry attractive fruit, they are eaten by birds even before ripening.

SORBUS The mountain ashes and whitebeams often have decorative berries, but on most species they are eaten at an early stage by birds. The following are usually exceptions: *S. cashmeriana*, large, glistening white, hanging late; *S. esserteauiana*, very large clusters of small scarlet, or in 'Flava', yellow fruit, hang-

1 Cercidiphyllum japonicum turns brilliant red and yellow in autumn.

2 Chamaecyparis lawsoniana 'Stewartii' has foliage tipped with gold.

3 Nyssa sylvatica, the tupelo, is bright red in autumn.

ing late; *S. hupehensis*, large clusters of small white fruit, turning pink, and hanging late; *S.* 'Joseph Rock' has amber-coloured, long-lasting berries; *S. sargentiana* has great clusters of small, orange-red berries.

Yellow or golden foliage

Included here are some trees which do not retain their exceptional colour throughout the entire season, but are attractive during the early part of the summer. All are cultivars that must be propagated vegetatively since they rarely come true from seed. When suckers arise from ground level they should be removed.

Broad-leaved

ACER CAPPADOCICUM 'AUREA' Deep yellow leaves on opening and again in autumn. *A. negundo* 'Auratum', golden-yellow foliage; *A. pseudoplatanus* 'Corstorphinense', the golden sycamore, has leaves changing from pale through rich yellow to green in late summer, makes a large tree. 'Worlei' has soft yellow leaves until late summer.
CATALPA BIGNONIOIDES 'AUREA' A small growing cultivar of the Indian bean tree with large golden leaves.
FAGUS SYLVATICA 'ZLATIA' A yellow-leaved beech
GLEDITSIA TRIACANTHOS 'SUN-BURST' This has bright yellow unfolding leaves.
ROBINIA PSEUDOACACIA 'FRISIA' This has golden-yellow leaves throughout.
ULMUS CARPINIFOLIA SARNIENSIS A slow-growing form of the Wheatley elm with pure golden coloured leaves. *U. glabra* 'Lutescens', a wych elm with pale yellow leaves; *U. procera* 'Vanhouttei', a golden-leaved form of hedgerow elm.

Conifers

CEDRUS DEODARA 'AUREA' The golden deodar, smaller than the type, is the best golden cedar.
CHAMAECYPARIS LAWSONIANA 'Lutea' Has golden-yellow foliage; 'Stewartii' is a free-growing yellow form; *C. obtusa* 'Crippsii' is good deep yellow, slowly reaching tree size.
CUPRESSUS MACROCARPA 'Donard Gold' a deep yellow and 'Lutea' paler yellow.
TAXUS BACCATA 'ELEGANTISSIMA' The golden yew; 'Fastigiata Aurea' is the golden Irish yew.

Blue and silver foliage
Broad-leaved
EUCALYPTUS The tree has numerous species, but their hardiness over a long period is doubtful; *E. gunnii* is the best known.
POPULUS ALBA The white poplar has white twigs and undersides of the leaves, the best form for the garden being the erect-growing 'Pyramidalis'. *P. canescens* has grey

leaves and makes a large, vigorously suckering tree.
SORBUS ARIA The whitebeam and all its cultivars have a persistent vivid, white underside to the leaves; in 'Lutescens' the upper surface also is creamy-white.
TILIA PETIOLARIS This has silvery undersides to the large, drooping leaves; in *T. tomentosa* the underneath is quite white.

Conifers

CEDRUS ATLANTICA GLAUCA A large tree with glaucous-blue, and in some specimens, almost silvery leaves.
CHAMAECYPARIS LAWSONIANA Includes a number of glaucous-blue foliaged cultivars including 'Allumii', 'Columnaris', 'Elegantissima', 'Erecta Alba', 'Fraseri', 'Glauca' (better known as 'Milford Blue Jacket'), 'Robusta Glauca', 'Silver Queen' (the foliage turning green in late summer) and 'Triomphe de Boskoop' (tending towards blue).
CUPRESSUS ARIZONICA 'Bonita' has very grey-blue foliage; in 'Pyramidalis' it is somewhat bluer.
JUNIPERUS CHINENSIS PYRAMIDALIS Has markedly blue foliage.
PICEA GLAUCA A large spruce with bluish-green leaves; *P. pungens* has grey-green

leaves, the cultivar 'Glauca' is smaller with grey-blue leaves and 'Moerheimii' is an even more intensely coloured form.

Variegated foliage

These are often sports (mutants) usually occurring originally on one branch only, of normal trees. However, some originate as the result of a virus infection.

The deciduous broad-leaved kinds are cheerful in urban areas where smoke pollution is not too bad, but the evergreen conifers on which the foliage persists for several years become drab. Most of these trees fit well into the normal colour scheme of a garden.

Broad-leaved

ACER NEGUNDO The box elder, provides excellent variegated foliage in 'Elegantissimum', bright yellow and 'Variegatum', conspicuously white.
ILEX AQUIFOLIUM A number of variegated leaved forms include 'Argenteomarginata', silver-variegated, berrying; 'Flavescens', moonlight holly, yellow and gold, berrying; 'Golden King', wide yellow margins, berrying; 'Golden Milkmaid', gold with narrow green margins, not berrying; 'Handsworth New Silver', dark green with white

margin, berrying; 'Madame Briot', leaves margined and blotched with gold, berrying; 'Silver Queen', bold creamy-white margins, not berrying.

LIRIODENDRON TULIPIFERA 'AUREA-MARGINATUM' A tulip tree with yellow-margined leaves making a large tree.

ULMUS PROCERA 'ARGENTEOVARIE-GATA' A hedgerow elm having leaves mottled with white.

Conifers

CHAMAECYPARIS LAWSONIANA 'ALBO-SPICA' The tips of branches creamy-white; 'Silver Queen', young foliage silver-white.

TAXUS BACCATA DOVASTONII 'AUREA' A golden variegated form of the weeping yew.

THUJA PLICATA 'ZEBRINA' A fine tree, smaller than the type, variegated with bright yellow.

TSUGA CANADENSIS 'ALBO-SPICA' The tree has white tips to the shoots.

Red and purple foliage

Placing trees of these colours needs great care, but their colours mingled with the multitude of others in autumn are effective and of great beauty, they do not blend well with the normal greens, particularly if used in quantity. They should therefore be used sparingly in isolation at points where they will inevitably catch the eye.

A number have clear colours when the leaves unfold but gradually lose this quality and become sombre as the season progresses. Others, not included here, become normal green when the leaves are open.

ACER PLATANOIDES 'Crimson King' ('Goldsworth Purple'), a Norway maple with

1 Cedrus atlantica 'Glauca' is a graceful conifer with ice-blue foliage.
2 One of the variegated forms of holly, Ilex aquifolium.
3 Fagus sylvatica purpurea, the purple beech, is a handsome tree for a large garden.

2

crimson-purple leaves larger than the type.

BETULA PENDULA 'PURPUREA' The purple-leaved birch is not a vigorous tree.

FAGUS SYLVATICA 'Riversii' the dark purple beech, and *purpurea*, purple and copper beech, are all well-known, reliable trees reaching a considerable size and quite unsuitable for other than the largest garden. Weeping forms of these coloured variants are also available.

MALUS The flowering crabs provide several kinds with red or purple foliage combined with gay flowers and decorative fruits. All are very hardy and adaptable, well suited to a small garden; M. X 'Aldenhamensis', purplish leaves, rich red flowers and crimson fruit. M. X 'Eleyi' is rather more vigorous than the last, the leaves bronze-green flushed with purple, the fruit hanging longer on the tree. M. X *purpurea* has dark purplish-green leaves, crimson flowers and fruits, both tinged with purple.

PRUNUS Several plums have coloured leaves, the best including P. X *blireana* (often a large shrub) deep copper with pink flowers. P. *cerasifera* 'Pissardii', with crimson-purple leaves, suitable also for hedging; 'Nigra' has darker leaves.

QUERCUS PETRAEA 'PURPUREA' Has

reddish-purple leaves which become green flushed with red. Q. *robur* 'Fastigiata Purpurea' has young leaves the same colour.

Trees with early flowers

ACER OPALUS The Italian maple has yellow flowers in early spring.

PARROTIA PERSICA This bears very numerous small dull scarlet tassell-like flowers at the end of winter.

PRUNUS 'Accolade' is a semi-double pink cherry flowering in early spring; P. *conradinae* is a cherry with scented white or pinkish flowers in late winter; P. *davidiana* is a peach flowering in winter. 'Alba' is a white form. P. 'Fudanzakura' ('Semperflorens') with pink buds and white flowers, all through winter. P. 'Kursar' a bright pink cherry flowering in late winter; P. 'Okami' a cherry with carmine-pink flowers in early spring; P. 'Pandora' is a single pink, very floriferous spring-flowering cherry, giving good autumnal leaf colour; P. *subhirtella* 'Autumnalis' carries semi-double white to pink flowers all through winter.

SALIX CAPREA The goat willow has decorative catkins in early spring; S. *daphnoides*, the violet-willow, carries them even earlier.

Evergreen trees

Broad-leaved

It is as well to remember that these often drop their leaves untidily in summer.

ARBUTUS All species and hybrids.

BUXUS All species and cultivars.

EUCALYPTUS All species.

ILEX I. X altaclarensis, I. aquifolium and their cultivars are evergreen hollies.

LIGUSTRUM LUCIDUM A species of privet often reaching tree size, has handsome dark green, glossy leaves, and white flowers in late summer.

MAGNOLIA DELAVAYI This and *M. grandiflora* are evergreens reaching tree size.

PHILLYREA LATIFOLIA A neglected, small evergreen tree with dense, dark-green, glossy foliage.

QUERCUS ILEX The holm oak and *Q. suber*, the cork oak, are handsome trees capable of reaching large sizes, the latter needing mild conditions.

Conifers

All conifers are evergreen with the exception of *Ginkgo, Larix* (larch), *Pseudolarix, Metasequoia* and *Taxodium* (swamp cypress).

Fastigiate trees

To the botanist, the word fastigiate means 'with parallel, erect, clustered branches'. It has now become more widely used in a more generalised sense for trees with narrow crowns. All those mentioned are derived from natural sports and do not come true from seed (if that is produced). They are propagated as cultivars. They generally need careful pruning when young to ensure the necessary erect growth.

Their placing needs great care, as they inevitably have an unnatural look, Fastigiate conifers accord well when planted in the regular pattern of formal gardens—the use of the true cypress in the great Italian gardens of the Renaissance. Fastigiate trees can be skilfully used, too, for adding a steadying vertical element to a steeply sloping site. The planting of a pair one on either side of the introduction to a vista can be very effective. Some of the less erect-growing are excellent for planting in narrow roads, or, for example, at the centre of a lawn where space is limited.

Broad-leaved

ACER SACCHARINUM 'PYRAMIDALE' An upright form of the silver maple, useful for street planting.

BETULA PENDULA 'FASTIGIATA' This is an erect, slow-growing form of the common birch, resembling an erect besom.

CARPINUS BETULUS 'FASTIGIATA' This is a valuable pyramidal rather than truly fastigiate cultivar of the hornbeam.

CRATAEGUS MONOGYNA 'STRICTA' This has a narrow, erect-growing crown.

FAGUS SYLVATICA 'FASTIGIATA' The

1

2

Dawyck beech is a good erect tree.

LIRIODENDRON TULIPIFERA 'FASTI-GIATUM' A narrow-growing form of the tulip tree.

MALUS HUPEHENSIS This has large white flowers and fairly erect growth. *M. prunifolia* 'Fastigiata', the fastigiate Siberian crab.

POPULUS ALBA 'PYRAMIDALIS' An erect-growing, very effective form of the white poplar; *P. nigra* 'Italica' is the common large-growing Lombardy poplar.

PRUNUS 'AMANOGAWA' A very fastigiate, small-growing cherry with double pink flowers; *P. hillieri* 'Spire' reaches 25ft (7.57m) with pink flowers and good autumn foliage; *P.* 'Umeniko' has single white flowers with leaves colouring in autumn.

QUERCUS ROBUR 'FASTIGIATA' The cypress oak, makes a broadly columnar tree of interesting form.

SORBUS AUCUPARIA 'FASTIGIATA' A particularly narrow form of the rowan.

ULMUS X SARNIENSIS The Wheatley elm is a large tree of flame-like form excellent for street planting; *U. glabra* 'Exoniensis' is a slow-growing erect form of the wych elm, the leaves often being distorted.

Conifers

CEDRUS ATLANTICA 'FASTIGIATA' A narrowly pyramidal form of the Atlas cedar.

CHAMAECYPARIS LAWSONIANA This provides a number of narrowly erect forms, including the popular 'Allumii' with bluish foliage; 'Columnaris' very narrow, glaucous blue; 'Erecta' bright green; 'Kilmacurragh', bright green; and 'Wissellii' a fine tree reaching considerable size.

X CUPRESSOCYPARIS LEYLANDII This is a densely-leaved, quick-growing tree of large size and fairly narrow shape.

CUPRESSUS GLABRA 'PYRAMIDALIS' This is very narrow, of moderate size and with almost grey foliage.

JUNIPERUS COMMUNIS 'HIBERNICA' The Irish juniper is columnar, but needs supporting.

LIBOCEDRUS DECURRENS The incense cedar is large and columnar.

TAXUS BACCATA 'FASTIGIATA' The well-known Irish yew of churchyards, the golden-leaved form being 'Fastigiata Aureomarginata'.

THUJA OCCIDENTALIS 'FASTIGIATA' A slow-growing, very narrow tree.

3

4

5

1 *Libocedrus decurrens*, the incense cedar, is distinctively columnar.
2 *Chamaecyparis lawsoniana 'Wisselli'* has a narrow fastigiate form.
3 *Ulmus glabra 'Pendula'* is the neatly-shaped weeping elm.
4 *Pyrus salicifolia 'Pendula'* is the dainty willow-leaved pear.
5 *Prunus subhirtella 'Pendula'* is the weeping spring cherry.

Weeping trees

Weeping trees are mostly natural sports that must be propagated as cultivars. They are difficult to place on account of their arresting form, and must stand in isolation since much of their beauty lies in the manner which their branches sweep down to the ground. Nothing should be grown under them.

Few trees are more frequently planted in an unsuitable place than the weeping willow, attractive when it is a small, slender tree, but becoming mighty in age, when its form often has to be damaged by savage pruning.

BETULA PENDULA 'TRISTIS' A graceful form of the silver birch with steeply drooping branches; 'Youngii' is smaller, more compact and slow-growing.

CARAGANA ARBORESCENS 'PENDULA' An attractive small weeping tree with yellow pea-shaped flowers and fern-like leaves.

CRATAEGUS MONOGYNA 'PENDULA' A weeping hawthorn; 'Pendula Rosea' has pink flowers.

FAGUS SYLVATICA 'PENDULA' The weeping beech, making a big tree.

FRAXINUS EXCELSIOR 'PENDULA' The well-known weeping ash.

GLEDITSIA TRIACANTHOS 'BUJOTI' ('PENDULA') A honey-locust with pendulous branches.

ILEX AQUIFOLIUM 'ARGENTEOMAR-GINATA PENDULA' Perry's silver weeping holly, berrying freely.

LABURNUM ANAGYROIDES 'PENDU-LUM' A gracefully weeping laburnum.

MALUS The following crab-apples have pendulous branches: *M.* 'Exzellenz Thiel', a small tree with crimson buds and pink flowers, floriferous but no fruit; *M. prunifolia* 'Pendula', the weeping Siberian crab, with numerous small, scarlet, persistent fruit; *M.* 'Elise Rathke', is probably a weeping form of the native crab.

MORUS ALBA 'PENDULA' The weeping white mulberry is a small tree with perpendicular branches, the fruit is insignificant.

PRUNUS PERSICA 'Windle Weeping' A weeping peach with double pink flowers; *P. subhirtella* 'Pendula', the weeping spring cherry, has very numerous pale pink flowers; *P. yedoensis* 'Shidare Yoshino' ('Perpendens') is a very pendulous form of the early Yoshino cherry.

PYRUS SALICIFOLIA 'PENDULA' A very pendulous form of the silver willow-leaved pear.

SALIX X CHRYSOCOMA (ALBA 'TRIS-TIS') The now common weeping willow, making a large tree; *S. babylonica* is rare and not satisfactory.

SOPHORA JAPONICA 'PENDULA' A small arbour-like tree with slender branchlets falling perpendicularly.

TILIA PETIOLARIS The weeping silver lime is a magnificent tree with a silvery sheen on the underside of the large leaves.

ULMUS GLABRA 'CAMPERDOWNII' The smaller of the two weeping wych elms with very pendulous branches, 'Pendula' being larger and more spreading in form.

Conifers

CHAMAECYPARIS NOOTKATENSIS 'PEN-DULA' a handsome, rather large tree with long drooping branches.

JUNIPERUS RECURVA COXII A moderate-sized, narrow tree with long, glaucous shoots drooping steeply.

PICEA BREWERIANA Brewer's weeping spruce, is a sombre tree with very long branchlets that hang vertically; *P. smithiana*, the Himalayan spruce, is a large tree with steeply drooping branchlets and exceptionally long leaves.

TAXUS BACCATA 'DOVASTONIANA' A yew with spreading branches from which the branchlets droop.

some popular trees

Acer

Old Roman name for hedgerow maple (*Aceraceae*). Deciduous trees, ranging in size from little more than shrubs (*A. palmatum* and its cultivars) to large trees (*A. pseudoplatanus*). Seeds winged, joined in pairs (keys). Buds opposite on twigs, thus differentiating the genus from *Platanus*. The flowers are usually insignificant. The trees are cultivated variously for their timber, foliage (particularly autumn colouring), or decorative 'snake-bark'. Many have free-running, sometimes sweet, watery sap.

Species cultivated

A. campestre, hedgerow or field maple, mostly used for hedges, but will reach 70ft (21.3m). Good on chalk. Burrs provide 'bird's-eye maple', Europe (including British Isles except Ireland), Asia. *A. capillipes*, to 30ft (9.1m), snake-bark white on green, leaves crimson in autumn, Japan. *A. cappadocicum* (syn. *laetum*), to 50ft (15.2m); cultivar 'Aureum' has yellow and 'Rubrum' red young foliage, all turn yellow in autumn, Caucasus. *A. davidii*, to 35ft (10.6m), snake-bark grey on green, varicoloured leaves in autumn, central China. *A. hersii* (syn. *grosseri hersii*) 25ft (7.6m), snakebark, white on green, good varied autumn colour, central China. *A. ginnala*, 10 to 20ft (3 to 6m), bushy, scarlet autumn leaves, China, Japan, Manchuria. *A. griseum*, paperbark maple, 35 to 40ft (9.1 to 12.2m), bark peels to show orange stem, good autumn colour, central China. *A. japonicum*, bushy to 25ft (7.6m), good autumn colour; cultivar 'Aureum' with yellow leaves, 'Aconitifolium' and 'Vitifolium', both with deeply cut leaves, Japan. *A. negundo*, box elder, 40 to 50ft (12.2 to 15.2m), leaves, resemble those of an ash; cultivar 'Auratum', golden leaves, 'Elegantissimum', yellow variegated leaves, 'Variegatum', prominently white variegated leaves, eastern North America. *A. opalus*, Italian maple, 30 to 60ft (9.1 to 18.3m), prominent yellow flowers, southern and central Europe. *A. palmatum*, Japanese maple, large bush or small tree with five-lobed leaves, Japan. Many cultivars including 'Atropurpureum', dull crimson, 'Crippsii', with finely cut red leaves, 'Dissectum', finely cut green leaves, 'Dissectum Atropurpureum', dull crimson, 'Heptalobum',

1 The leaves of Acer pseudoplatanus are pink in early spring.
2 Aesculus hippocastanum, the common horsechestnut, produces nuts called conkers.

coral-red shoots. *A. pensylvanicum*, 20 to 30ft has seven-lobed leaves and cultivars 'Osaka-zuki', brilliant autumn colouring, 'Senkaki', coral-red shoots. *A. pensylvanicum*, 20 to 30ft (6 to 9.1m), snake-bark, white on green, yellow autumn colour, easter North America; *A. platanoides*, Norway maple, 60 to 80ft (18.3 to 24.4m), timber tree, yellow flowers, good autumn colour, very hardy. Cultivars include 'Crimson King', crimson-purple leaves, 'Drummondii', leaves white border, 'Laciniatum', eagle's-claw maple, small leaves, 'Reitenbachii', red leaves when young, 'Schwedleri', crimson-purple when young, continental Europe. *A. pseudoplatanus*, sycamore (plane in Scotland), 60 to 100ft (18.3 to 30.4m), timber and shelter tree of great hardiness; the cultivars, usually smaller, include 'Brilliantissimum', leaves coral-pink in spring, becoming normal, 'Corstorphin-ense', Corstorphine plane, leaves pale yellow at first, then golden, finally green in late summer, 'Leopoldii', cream and white variegation, *purpureum*, leaves purple underneath, 'Spaethii', an improved *purpureum*, 'Worleyi', an improved 'Corstorphinense', Europe. *A. rubrum*, red American maple, 60 to 80ft (18.3 to 24.4m), red flowers before leaves, eastern North America. *A. rufinerve*, 25ft (7.6m), blue-white shoots; *A. saccharinum* (syn. *dasycarpum*), silver maple, 60 to 85ft (18.3 to 25.9m), leaves silvery underneath; cultivars are 'Laciniatum', leaves more deeply cut, 'Pyramidale', erect-growing form.

Cultivation

All maples grow best in a fertile, moisture retentive, but well drained soil. Of the species here described, *A. japonicum* and *palmatum* thrive best in a neutral to acid soil, although satisfactory growth can be obtained on limy soils by digging in peat or leaf-mould. These two maples and *A. pensylvanicum* thrive in sun or shade, the remainder are best in a sunny site. Propagation is by seeds sown when ripe either outside in nursery rows or in pots in a cold frame, transplanting the seedlings to nursery rows later. Protection from mice may be necessary. Cultivars such as *A. negundo* 'Variegatum' and *A. platanoides* 'Drummondii' do not come from seed and are grafted onto seedlings of the original species.

Aesculus

The old Latin name for a tree, not, however, of this genus, whose members were not known until the mid-seventeenth century (*Hippo-castanaceae*). Mostly large trees grown for their handsome panicles of flowers, followed by seeds (conkers) in more or less spiny cases. All have palmate leaves. European species are called horse-chestnuts, North American species are known as buckeyes.

Species cultivated

A. X carnea, pink horse-chestnut, 60 to 80ft

Araucaria araucana, the monkey puzzle or Chile pine, is a large and unusual coniferous evergreen tree from South America. Unlike others of the genus it is generally hardy and can attain an enormous height when grown naturally.

(18.3 to 24.4m), hybrid between *A. hippo-castanum* and *A. pavia*, rosy-pink flowers spring; cultivars include 'Briotii' with redder flowers. *A. hippocastanum*, horse-chestnut, 90 to 125ft (27.4 to 38m), white flowers spring, introduced early seventeenth century, cultivar 'Baumanii' has double flowers and does not bear conkers, Albania and north Greece. *A. indica*, Indian horse-chestnut, 60 to 80ft (18.3 to 24.4m), similar to *hippocastanum*, but with longer, narrower leaves and larger panicles, flowering in summer, north-west Himalayas. *A. parviflora*, dwarf buckeye, spreading shrub to 10ft (3m), with many white flowers in late summer and early autumn, south-east USA. *A. pavia*, red-buckeye, small tree with crimson flowers in summer, fruit smooth and spineless, southern USA.

Cultivation

A. hippocastanum and its hybrids are most adaptable trees. All species will grow on limestone and chalk. Propagation is by seeds sown as soon as possible after ripening as they soon lose their viability. Cultivars should be

budded or grafted, though *A. X carnea* comes more or less true from seed.

Araucaria

Named after the Araucanos, a tribe of Indians in Chile, the home of *A. araucana* (*Araucariaceae*). Large, evergreen, coniferous trees, only one of which, *A. araucana*, is generally hardy. Others are cultivated in temperate houses where they cannot achieve their full status of 150ft (45.7m) or more. Male and female flowers are normally carried on separate trees.

Species cultivated

A. araucana (syn. *A. imbricata*) monkey puzzle or Chile pine, 70 to 85ft (21.3 to 25.9m), a hardy tree of remarkable appearance, male and female trees must adjoin to produce the large seed, in Chile eaten after boiling, as dessert, Chile.

Cultivation

A. araucana thrives best in moist, fertile soils in the milder parts of the temperate zone; is quite unsuitable for the small garden. Propagation is by seeds sown in pots in spring either with or without heat. Protection is needed for two years; then seedlings may be planted out in late spring, watering them well.

17

Betula

This name was the Latin for the common birch (*Betulaceae*). Small or moderate sized, slender, deciduous trees, many coming from high altitudes or cold climates and so extremely hardy. In a number of species the bark is attractively coloured. The free-flowing watery sap of some species of this tree was once used for making beer.

Species cultivated

B. albo-sinensis septentrionalis, 40 to 50ft (12.2 to 15.2m), trunk shining orange-brown to orange-yellow, western China. *B. papyrifera*, paper or canoe birch, 60 to 80ft (18.3 to 24.4m), gleaming white bark with rather large leaves; bark was used for canoes and containers, north-east America. *B. pendula* (syn. *verrucosa*), silver birch, 50 to 100ft (15.2 to 30.4m), white bark, in spite of name not always pendulous, twigs rough with minute warts. Cultivars include 'Dalecarlica', Swedish birch, with cut leaves and pendulous branches; 'Fastigiata', erect growing form; 'Youngii', Young's weeping birch, a small tree with very pendulous branches, Europe (including British Isles), Asia Minor.

Cultivation

Birches normally grow on light soil in airy conditions, all will thrive in average garden soils provided they do not dry out excessively. Propagation is by seed sown in early spring scarcely covered with soil – and carefully kept moist – which sometimes germinates badly. Cultivars must be grafted or budded onto the species.

Chamaecyparis

From the Greek *chamai*, on the ground, and *kuparissos*, cypress (i.e. dwarf cypress), indicating the affinity of this genus to the true cypresses (*Cupressus*) in which genus they were formerly, and are by some nurserymen still included. Some species also formerly called *Retinospora* (*Pinaceae*). False cypresses. Evergreen, erect trees, natives of north America, Japan and Formosa, with scale-like leaves forming flattened shoots in fern-like sprays, the leaders usually nodding. Male and female flowers, very small (the males sometimes so numerous as to give the trees a crimson glow) on the same tree. Cones small, globular.

Species cultivated

C. lawsoniana, Lawson cypress, hardy, a narrow tree, 100ft (30.4m), often producing more than one leader, used in forestry but principally grown for ornamental purposes; cultivars include 'Albo-spica', pyramid, branches tipped creamy-white; 'Allumii', 40ft (12.2m), forms a dense column, glaucous blue; 'Columnaris', 40ft (12.2m), narrow with

Arbutus

The Roman name for the strawberry tree (*Ericaceae*). Evergreen trees, or in cold situations large shrubs, noted for their lily-of-the-valley flowers, roundish orange-red (not very strawberry-like) fruit, and attractive foliage. They are fairly hardy and are among the few ericaceous trees that will grow on chalk.

Species cultivated

A. andrachne, Grecian strawberry tree, 10 to 20ft (3 to 6m), flowers in early spring, the trunk cinnamon-red, young plants tender and needing winter protection, but in mild districts or when carefully sited becoming hardy, south-eastern Europe. *A. X andrachnoides* (syn. *hybrida*), 15 to 20ft (4.5 to 6m), a natural hybrid between *A. andrachne* and *A. unedo*, quite hardy with striking cinnamon-red trunk and

1 The red bark of Arbutus X andrachnoides, one of the strawberry trees.
2 Betula pendula youngii, Young's weeping birch.

branches, flowers in late autumn or spring. *A. unedo*, the strawberry tree, 15 to 40ft (4.5 to 12.2m), hardy, flowers and ripe fruits borne together in autumn, the latter soon consumed by birds, Mediterranean region, western France, Ireland.

Cultivation

Arbutuses are best raised under glass from imported seed (though home-grown seed of *A. unedo* is fertile) which germinates freely. Pot up as soon as possible, potting on and keeping under glass two or three years, then planting direct into permanent position. Protect in winter until established.

1 Chamaecyparis lawsoniana allumii grows in a tall dense column.
2 Davidia involucrata, the handkerchief tree, is enchanting, attractive and hardy. Sometimes also referred to as the Dove tree or ghost tree, it grows to 50 feet and flowers in May. Cultivate in a sheltered position.

glaucous foliage; 'Ellwoodii', 15ft (4.5m), pyramid, blue-grey foliage, slow-growing; 'Erecta' (syn. 'Erecta Viridis'), 80ft (24.4m), vigorous, narrow, bright green; 'Fletcheri', 15ft (4.5m), small, narrow with feathery blue-grey foliage; 'Fraseri', 40ft (12.2m), narrow, grey-green foliage; 'Kilmacurragh', recently introduced, very upright and narrow, bright green foliage; 'Pottenii', slow-growing, conical, feathery green foliage; 'Triomphe de Boskoop', 70ft (21.3m), vigorous-growing, broad pyramid, glaucous-blue foliage; 'Wissellii', 70ft (21.3m), vigorous, narrow column with densely crowded branches and blue-green foliage, western North America. *C. nootkatensis* (syn. *Thujopsis borealis*), Nootka cypress, 90ft (27.4m), but slow-growing, resembling *lawsoniana*, but with foliage more pendulous and hook-like projections on cone scales; cultivars 'Pendula', very pendulous, a remarkable variation, Pacific coast of North America. *C. obtusa* (syn. *Retinospora obtusa*), Hinoki, 70ft (21.3m), slower growing than either of the foregoing, of stiffer habit and with blunt-pointed leaves; cultivars include 'Crippsii', 30ft (9.1m), slow-growing with golden foliage; 'Tetragona', 15ft (4.5m), small tree or shrub; 'Tetragona Aurea', golden leaved, Japan. *C. pisifera* (syn. *Retinospora pisifera*), Sawara cypress, 50 to 70ft (15.2 to 21.3m), a moderate-sized, narrow pyramid tree, of more open growth than the

Hinoki, cones very small; cultivars 'Aurea', golden-leaved; 'Filifera', 50ft (15.2m), with cord-like foliage; 'Plumosa', 60ft (18.3m), grey-green feathery foliage; 'Squarrosa', 50ft (15.2m), with more open foliage than 'Plumosa', Japan.

Cultivation

Ordinary soil is adequate, the majority growing satisfactorily on lime and chalk soils. All grow to greater heights in warmer parts of the temperate region with a good rainfall. Plant when young in their permanent positions. Propagation of the species is by seed, which is freely produced and should be sown in autumn where greenhouse protection is available, otherwise in spring. The cultivars can mostly be reproduced from cuttings taken in late summer, or by grafting on to the species.

Davidia

Commemorating Father J. P. A. David (1826–1900), French missionary and pioneer naturalist in China and Tibet (*Davidiaceae*). Dove tree, pocket-handkerchief tree, ghost tree. A genus of a single species, *D. involucrata*, a hardy deciduous tree to 50ft (15.2m), bearing in spring small insignificant flowers carried between two white bracts, one 6ins (152mm) long, which gives it the popular names; the form *vilmoriniana* has smooth leaves which show off the flowers better than the downy underside of the leaves of the type, central and western China.

Cultivation

This attractive tree requires a sheltered position in ordinary soils, including those containing lime. Propagation is by the large, nut-like seeds which must be exposed to the winter weather and often take 2 or 3 years to germinate, or by cutting from half-ripe wood in late summer, or by hardwood cuttings in late autumn.

Fagus

The name is the ancient Latin for the common beech (*Fagaceae*). A small genus of deciduous trees, including valuable timber producers. The fruit, known as 'mast', is a sharp-edged triangular nut in a rough husk.

Species cultivated

F. sylvatica, common beech, large tree to 140ft (42.7m), with spreading flattened branch system, much grown for timber and principally for joiner's work, and chairs. The nuts are edible and eaten by animals (including domestic) and birds. A typical tree of chalk hills and downs, Europe, including Britain. Varieties are numerous; they include: 'Fastigiata', Dawyck beech, slow-growing fastigiate form; 'Laciniata', beautiful cut-leaved (fern-leaf) form; 'Pendula', weeping beech; 'Purpurea', purple and copper leaved forms; 'Purpurea-Pendula', weeping purple beech; 'Riversii', a good form of purple beech.

Cultivation

The common beech thrives on well-drained light soils, especially on lime. It is good for hedges, the brown dead leaves hanging till spring. For hedging purposes plant 9ins (229mm) apart, cutting the sides hard but not the leaders until the required height is reached. Propagation is from seeds sown 1in

1 *Halesia carolina*, the snowdrop tree.
2 *Fagus sylvatica*, the common beech.
3 *Fraxinus excelsior* 'Pendula'.

(25.4mm) deep in rows 18ins (45.8mm) apart in spring. Transplant seedlings in their second year. The varieties are propagated by grafting in spring on to the common species.

Fraxinus

The ancient Latin name for the common ash (*Oleaceae*). A genus mainly of large deciduous trees with pinnate leaves and numerous minute flowers before the leaves open, followed by winged fruits (keys). They are widely distributed over the Northern Hemisphere.

Species cultivated

F. americana, white ash, tree to 8oft (24.4m), quick-growing, handsome timber tree, eastern U.S.A. *F. excelsior*, common ash, large tree to 140 ft (42.7m), producing valuable timber used for tool handles, sports goods etc., common in British woods, Europe and Caucasus; cultivars 'Jaspidea Aurea', golden-barked ash, leaves yellow at fall; 'Pendula' weeping ash, branches drooping. *F. ornus*, manna or flowering ash, tree to 75ft (22.9m), strongly scented whitish flowers produced abundantly in late spring, south Europe and Asia Minor. *F. oxycarpa*, tree to 7oft (21.3m), leaves small, graceful tree, south Europe and Asia Minor; 'Raywood' is a cultivar with reddish-purple leaves in autumn. *F. pensylvanica*, red ash, tree to 4oft (12.2m), large leaves, eastern North America.

Cultivation

Ordinary, well-drained soils, including lime and gravel are suitable. Ornamental kinds are suitable for towns. Propagation is by seed which germinates more quickly if it is collected from trees and sown while green. If it is collected when brown it must be kept moist in peat or sand and sown in the following spring. Cultivars are grafted on to common species in early spring.

Ginkgo

Origin of name doubtful (*Ginkgoaceae*). Maidenhair tree. There is one species only, *G. biloba*, from China, a large deciduous, hardy tree with fan-shaped leaves and evil-smelling fruit like a small plum, though fruits are often not borne. The tree is a survivor from prehistoric times. Male and female flowers are borne on separate trees. This tree may grow to 90ft (27.4m), and is good for town planting. The leaves turn a good yellow in autumn before falling; cultivars 'Fastigiata', more upright in growth, a useful street tree; 'Pendula' is a small weeping form.

Cultivation

Ginkgo biloba will grow in any ordinary well-drained soil, including those that contain lime. Trees do best where they have a certain amount of shelter, rather than in completely exposed situations. Plant during winter. Propagation is from imported seed or by cuttings, of half-ripe wood in late summer, or dormant wood in winter.

Halesia

Commemorating the Rev. Stephen Hales (1677–1761), botanist (*Styracaceae*). Silver-bell or snowdrop trees. A small genus of hardy, small, deciduous trees, with pretty bell-shaped, usually white flowers.

Species cultivated

H. carolina (syn. *H. tetraptera*), Snowdrop tree, to 30ft (9.1m), white flowers, late spring, North America. *H. monticola*, similar to *H. carolina*, but stronger growing, to 100ft (30.4m) in the wild, lower growing in cultivation, with large flowers, mountains of south-eastern U.S.A., cultivar 'Rosea', pale rose flowers.

Cultivation

These trees prefer sandy loam, but will grow in other soils. Plant during winter. Prune only to shape, after flowering. They are propagated by seeds sown in spring, by root cuttings in spring or autumn, or by layering shoots in autumn.

The magnificent Ginkgo biloba, the maidenhair tree from China, is a fine street tree with attractive fan-shaped leaves.

Malus

From the Latin word for apple-tree (*Rosaceae*). Apple, crab apple. A genus of about 25 species, mostly hardy deciduous, rarely semi-evergreen, small or moderate in size, very twiggy trees or large bushes, cultivated primarily for their fruit but species (usually called crab-apples) and their cultivars grown for the beauty of their flowers, foliage or small, brightly-coloured fruit. The species and hybrids described below are all deciduous. All flower in spring.

Species cultivated

M. X 'Aldenhamensis'. 15ft (4.5m) rosy-crimson flowers, purplish leaves and fruits, hybrid. *M. X atrosanguinea*, 15 to 20ft (4.5 to 6m), rosy-crimson, hybrid. *M. baccata*, 40 to 50ft (12.2 to 15.2m), flowers white, eastern Asia; var. *mandschurica*, flowers white, fragrant, fruits red, the size of cherries. *M. coronaria* 'Charlottae', 25 to 30ft (7.6 to 9.1m), late flowering, semi-double, soft pink, large leaves colouring in autumn, garden origin. 'Dartmouth' white, fruits large, plum-like, covered with a purplish-red bloom. *M. X* 'Eleyi', to 20ft (6m), wine-red flowers, purplish leaves, numerous small purple-red fruits, hybrid. *M. floribunda*, Japanese crab, to 30 ft (9.1m), arching branches with numerous carmine flower buds opening to white, small red fruit, probably Japan. 'Golden Hornet', erect to 25ft (7.6m) white flowers, prolific yellow, cherry-sized fruit. *M. X hillieri*, to 20 ft (6m), arching branches, semi-double pink flowers, crimson in bud, hybrid origin. *M. hupehensis* (syn. *M. theifera*), Hupeh crab, large white flowers, orange-pink in bud, in autumn, numerous small, orange-red cherry-like fruits, Western China. 'John Downie', vigorous tree to 35ft (10.6m), inverted pear-shaped fruits, yellow, flushed red, good cooking crab, garden origin. *M. X* 'Lemoinei', erect growing, large wine-coloured single flowers, small red fruit, hybrid origin. *M. X* 'Magdeburgensis', small tree, flowers rose, semi-double, hybrid. *M. X micromalus*, small tree, flowers pink and white, hybrid. 'Profusion', vigorous growth, young leaves at first copper-crimson, flowers wine-red, large, in clusters of six or seven, garden origin. *M. prunifolia*, small tree, flowers white, numerous red fruits hanging long on tree, Eastern Asia; cultivars 'Cheal's Crimson', good form with crimson fruits; 'Fastigiata', erect growth; 'Pendula', weeping form. *M. niedzwetzkyana*, reddish leaves, flowers purple-red, clustered, fruits large, dark red covered with purplish bloom, much used in hybridisation. *M. X purpurea*, rather spreading small tree, rosy-crimson flowers, dark purplish-green shoots and leaves, numerous dull crimson fruits, hybrid origin. *M. robusta*, Siberian crab, cherry apple, vigorous round-headed small tree, white flowers, fruit prolific, cherry-like; cultivars 'Red Siberian', fruits red; 'Yellow Siberian', fruits yellow; all hybrid origin. *M. tschonoskii*, 30 to 40ft (9.1 to 12.2m), pyramidal habit, flowers white flushed pink, fruits to 1in (25.4mm) wide, brownish-yellow, good autumn leaf colour, Japan. 'Wisley Crab', vigorous tree, bronzy-red leaves, flowers wine-coloured, fruit large, shiny red, garden origin. *M. yunnanensis*, 20 to 40ft (6 to 12.2m), flowers white or pale pink, fruits small, red, good autumn colour; var. *veitchii*, bright-coloured fruits.

Cultivation

The decorative species and hybrid crabs are tolerant of a wide range of soils, are extremely hardy and flower regularly, many kinds producing regular heavy crops of fruit. Only the minimum of pruning to shape the trees is necessary. They may be planted in sunny places among other trees or shrubs or make excellent specimen trees. Propagation of the hybrids and named kinds is by budding or grafting. The species may be raised from seeds, sown out of doors 3 ins (76.2mm) deep in sandy soil in late autumn, by cuttings 8 to 12ins (203 to 305mm) long rooted out of doors in autumn, or by layering in autumn.

1 The erect-growing Malus 'Lemoinei' has large wine-coloured single flowers, followed by small red fruits. Like most of the genus of about 25 species, it is deciduous.
2 The cherry-like red fruits of Malus robusta 'Red Siberian', the cherry apple. M. r. 'Yellow Siberian' produces golden fruits.

Morus

The ancient Latin name for the black mulberry (*Moraceae*). Mulberry. A genus of about 12 species of which those cultivated are hardy deciduous trees with insignificant catkin-like greenish flowers in spring.

Species cultivated

M. nigra, strikingly picturesque, often leaning, tree to 40ft (12.2m), grown for its edible, juicy fruit nearly black when ripe in late summer, central China.

Cultivation

Give the mulberry a fertile soil in a sunny situation. The male and female catkins are usually borne on the same tree of *M. nigra* so, where fruit is required a separate male tree

is not necessary. Plant in early summer, and prune only to shape. Propagation of species is by seed, or of the fruiting forms of *M. nigra*, by cuttings 12ins (305mm) or more long, taken in late winter and rooted in sandy soil.

Parrotia

After E. W. Parrot (1792–1841) a German naturalist and traveller, the first man to climb Mt Ararat (*Hamamelidaceae*). There is one species only in this genus, *P. persica*, a deciduous small, spreading tree to 30ft (9.1m) The bark of the trunk flakes like that of a plane tree, and it has flowers composed of numerous dull red stamens in early spring before the leaves. The leaves are more or less oblong, up to 5ins (127mm) long, resembling those of *Hamamelis*, and have the merit of turning in autumn to brilliant shades ranging from yellow to crimson. The fruit is nut-like. Parrotia is a native of Persia.

1 The mulberry, Morus nigra, makes a tall, full-headed tree when mature.
2 The spreading hardy Parrotia persica is grown mainly for the brilliant yellows and crimsons of its autumn leaves. This tree does not like lime soil or chalky ground.

Cultivation

This tree is very hardy but does not do well on limy soils, and is unsuited to chalk. It tends to make a sprawling shrub unless it is pruned to make a standard, which then shows the handsome bark to advantage; otherwise no pruning is needed. Plant in autumn or winter. Propagation is by layering shoots in autumn, or by seed, sown in pots of sandy soil and placed in the cold frame, in autumn or spring. Cuttings of ripened shoots may be rooted in autumn.

Picea

From the Latin *pix*, pitch or resin, on account of the resinous nature of the genus (*Pinaceae*). Spruce trees. A genus of about 50 species of evergreen trees, usually with pointed crowns, mostly growing in cool districts and on the high mountains of Europe, Asia Minor, Asia from the Himalaya north to Siberia, Japan and North America. Many are valuable timber trees and from others pitch and resin are produced. A number are of ornamental value. The pollen-bearing flowers are catkin-like, those developing seed resemble small cones; both sexes are usually found on the same tree. The leaves arise from distinct peg-like growths on the shoots and are usually stiff with sharp or hard points. The cones, of leathery texture,

are always more or less pendent so that when the scales part on ripening the winged seeds fall out and drift away, the cones hanging on the tree for a while until they fall entire. A help to classification is that the species can be divided into three groups according to the cross-sections of the leaves and the white markings (bands of stomata or minute orifices in the leaf surfaces) on them. These are (A) regularly quadrangular, with white bands on all four surfaces; (B) leaves unequally quadrangular, flattened, the wide upper and lower surfaces with white bands; the narrower edge surfaces without them; and (C) leaves flattened, the white bands usually only on the upper surface, the lower being green.

Species cultivated

The type of leaf is indicated by the letter in parentheses, as above. *P. abies* (syn. *excelsa*) (A), common spruce, tall tree, 110ft (33.5m) or more, leaves ½ to 1in (12.7 to 25.4mm) long, with blunt, horny point, shoots usually without hairs, cones 4 to 6ins (102 to 152mm) long. The common spruce is extensively grown both as a timber tree and for pulp. When small, it is the true Christmas tree; it is also a source of pitch and turpentine, central and northern Europe. *P. breweriana* (C), Brewer's weeping spruce, a distinctive tree up to 50ft (15.2m) in cultivation, the slender branchlets falling steeply and up to 8ft (2.4m) long, leaves blunt-tipped, dark green, up to 1¼ins (31.7mm) long, young shoots with greyish hairs, cones at first green, purple when ripening, finally brown, distinctively narrowing at each end, up to 5ins (127mm) long, a very rare mountain tree in south-western Oregon and north-western California only. *P. glauca* (A), white spruce, up to 100ft (30.4m) in cultivation, leaves pale green, curved, with horny point, ½in (12.7mm) long, shoots greyish at first becoming brown, cones blunt up to 2½ins (63.5mm) long, green becoming pale brown, Canada and northern United States where it is an important forest tree. *P. mariana* (A), black spruce, to 70ft (21.3m) in cultivation, leaves bluish-green, ½in (12.7mm) long with horny point, cones numerous and persistent, short stalked 1 to 1½ins (25.4 to 38.1mm) long, purplish at first, reddish-brown when ripe, Canada and north-eastern United States. *P. omorika* (C), Serbian spruce, a tree of strikingly narrow, sharply pointed form reaching 90ft (27.4m) in cultivation, leaves ½ to ¾ins (12.7 to 19mm) long, shining green above, grey below, young shoots light brown, cones up to 2ins (50.8mm) long, a bluish-black to dark brown, Yugoslavia. *P. orientalis* (A), oriental spruce, narrowly pyramidal, exceeding 100ft (30.4m) in cultivation, leaves very short ¼ to ½in (6.35 to 12.7mm) long, dark green, shining, very hairy, cones narrow up to 4 ins (102mm) long, purple becoming brown, mountains of Asia Minor, Armenia, Caucasus. *P. pungens* (A),

blue or Colorado spruce, reaching 80ft (24.4m) in cultivation, leaves curved, stout, prickly, bluish-green, young shoots stout, bluish-green at first becoming orange, cones up to 4ins (102mm) long, reddish-green becoming shiny brown when ripe; vars. *glauca* and 'Moerheimii' are particularly blue cultivars, smaller than the main type, western North America. *P. sitchensis* (B), Sitka spruce, a large tree exceeding 100ft (30.4m) in cultivation, leaves up to ¾in (19mm) long, bright green above, grey below, rigid and prickly, cones light brown, up to 4ins (102mm) long with papery scales, widely grown in British forestry, western borders of North America. *P. smithiana* (syn. *P. morinda*) (A), western Himalayan spruce, a distinctive tree exceeding 100ft (30.4m) in cultivation with drooping branchlets, leaves dark green, curved, slender, tapering to a horny point, the shoots pale brown, shining, without hairs,

Picea pungens glauca is a handsome evergreen.

cones up to 7ins (178mm) long, brown when ripe, western Himalaya.

Cultivation

These trees prefer a moist climate and fairly fertile ground; they do not usually thrive on thin, dry or chalky soils. Propagation is by seed, the cones being collected before they open and placed in a warm, dry place when in due course the seeds may be extracted and sown ⅛in (3.17mm) deep at the end of winter in a soil mixture of sand and loam in a cold frame or greenhouse, or out of doors in spring. In forestry, the seedlings are transplanted to their permanent positions when they are 9 to 12ins (229 to 305mm) tall; for planting in gardens they are usually grown on until they are 3 to 4ft (0.9 to 1.2m) tall before they are planted in their final positions.

Pinus

The ancient Latin name for the pine tree (*Pinaceae*). Pine. A genus of about 80 species, mostly trees though some are shrubs, widely distributed throughout the northern hemisphere. All are evergreen. The branches are arranged round the trunk in tiers, the leaves are of two kinds, small and often only scale-like, and the slender needle-shaped ones that are prominent and typical of the genus, arranged in bundles of 2, 3 or 5 held together, at least at first, within a basal sheath. The number of leaves is virtually consistent within a species and is stated below within brackets following the botanical name. The pollen-bearing flowers are catkin-like, those bearing seed like small cones; both are found on the same tree. The cones are woody, more or less pendent, from which the winged seeds fall and are distributed when the scales part; in some species, the cones remain attached to the shoots for many years and may open only from the heat of forest fires. The genus includes species producing valued timber, turpentine, and rosin; the seeds of some are edible. Many are ornamental.

Species cultivated

P. ayacahuite (5), Mexican white pine, 80ft (24.4m) or more in cultivation, branches horizontal, leaves 4 to 8in (102 to 203mm) long, bluish-green, young shoots brown or greyish, covered with down, cones borne singly or in clusters, 8 to 18in (203 to 457mm) long, to 3½in (88.9mm) wide at base, scales resinous, Mexico. *P. nigra* (syn. *P. austriaca*) (2), Austrian pine, rough, unshapely, heavily branched tree exceeding 100ft (30.4m) in cultivation, leaves stiff, stout, brittle, usually twisted, with horny points, 4 to 6in (102 to 152mm) long, young shoots ridged, yellowish-brown, without down, cones 2 to 3in (50.8 to 76.2mm) long, Austria, Yugoslavia and Hungary; commonly planted for ornament and windbreaks in British Isles; var. *maritima* (syn. *P. calabrica*) (2), Corsican pine, erect, regularly-branched tree otherwise resembling the foregoing, often exceeding 100ft (30.4m) in cultivation, leaves flexible, Spain, Corsica, southern Italy, Greece. *P. pinaster* (2), cluster or maritime pine, trunk of old trees usually bare of branches, reaching 100ft (30.4m) in cultivation, leaves deep green, stout, rigid, curved, apex horny, 5 to 6in (127 to 152mm) long, young shoots pale brown without down, becoming prominently ribbed, cones often produced in clusters, shining brown, 3 to 7in (76.2 to 178mm) long, Mediterranean region. *P. pinea* (2), stone pine, tree to 60ft (18.3m) in cultivation, with distinctive rounded crown, leaves straight but twisted, slender, grass-green, 4 to 6in (102 to 152mm) long, young shoots grey-green, without down, cones shining brown, up to 6in (152mm) long and 4in (102mm) broad, containing large edible seeds (piñons), Mediterranean region. *P.*

radiata (syn. *P. insignis*) (3), Monterey pine, a large quick-growing tree that has reached 140ft (42.7m) in England, leaves grow densely on shoots, grass-green, slender, curved, up to 6in (152mm) long, cones broad, asymmetrical, to 6in (152mm) long, remaining ringed round the branches for many years, native of a very limited area on Monterey peninsula, not hardy in the colder parts of the temperate regions. *P. strobus* (5), Weymouth or white pine, exceeding 100ft (30.4m) in cultivation, leaves dense, straight, slender, bluish-green, up to 5in (127mm) long but usually shorter, young shoots slender, green with tufts of hair at the base of the leaves, cones slender, curved, up to 6in (152mm) long, native of a wide area in Canada and the northern United States. *P. sylvestris* (2), Scots pine, tree up to 120ft (36.6m), with flat-tipped crown, bark of upper part red or orange, peeling in thin layers, leaves variable, twisted, rigid, grey-green, 1 to 4in (25.4 to 102mm) long, young shoots smooth, greenish, cones greyish-brown, 1 to 3in (25.4 to 76.2mm) long, borne singly or in clusters of from 2 to 3, native of Europe northwards to Siberia, including Scotland, extensively planted for timber production and ornament; cultivars 'Aurea', slow-growing, winter foliage golden. *P. wallichiana* (syn. *P. excelsa*) (5), Bhutan pine, reaching 100ft (30.4m) in cultivation, leaves spreading or drooping, often with a kink, sharp-pointed, greyish-green, 5 to 8in (127 to 203mm) long, young shoots bluish-green, without down, cones very resinous, rather slender with large scales, light brown, up to 12in (305mm) long, Afghanistan to Nepal, Bhutan.

Cultivation

Pines are light-loving trees and require well-drained soil; some, such as the Scots, Austrian and Corsican thrive on light and, within limits, on alkaline soils. All dislike polluted urban atmospheres. They are wind firm, and the commoner kinds make good wind-breaks. With the exception of those stated to come from warm localities, they are hardy. Propagation is by seeds, home-produced or imported. Seedlings have weak root systems and unless they are grown in pots they must be lifted in their second year, their roots trimmed and immediately replanted in nursery beds for 1 or 2 more years before planting out. Alternatively they may be undercut. It is important not to damage the leading bud.

Platanus

From the old Greek name for *P. orientalis*, derived from *platys*, broad, referring to the wide leaves (*Platanaceae*). Plane tree. A genus of 8 or 9 species of deciduous trees with lobed leaves borne alternately on the shoots, distinguishing them from those of maples (*Acer*) which are opposite. The seed-heads are ball-

Pinus sylvestris 'Beuvronensis' is a popular dwarf-growing conifer. Also known as the dwarf Scots pine, it makes a bushy ornamental plant for the garden.

like, either solitary or strung on slender stalks in groups of two to six. The thin bark peels off the trunks in irregular plates to disclose pale coloured inner bark. They are natives of Asia, North America and Mexico. One species only and a hybrid are normally found in the British Isles.

Species cultivated

P. orientalis, oriental plane, a handsome spreading tree reaching a great size, to 100ft (30.4m), the lower branches of old trees usually resting on the ground. The leaves are deeply lobed, and the fruiting balls are in groups of two to six on each chain, south-eastern Europe and Asia Minor. *P. X hispanica* (syn. *P. acerifolia*), London plane, is believed to be a hybrid and is extensively planted. Its origin is unknown but it was grown in the British Isles in the late seventeenth century. Heights exceeding 100ft (30.4m) are recorded.

Cultivation

P. orientalis must be raised from imported seed; cuttings are difficult to root. *P. X hispanica* strikes readily from cuttings of dormant wood or can be raised from seed borne on British trees. Both are hardy and will thrive in fertile soils of any kind, though they dislike dryness at the roots. They may be planted in suitable weather at any time in winter. If pruning is necessary, for shaping, this should be done in winter.

Populus

From the Latin *arbor populi*, tree of the people, of the Romans, the Lombardy poplar being much planted in the cities (*Salicaceae*). A genus of deciduous, usually fast-growing trees with about 35 species, and numerous hybrids propagated as cultivars. The flowers are in catkins, the male (with red anthers) and the female (green) on separate trees, pollination occurring before or with the unfolding of the leaves. They are distributed over North America, Europe, North Africa, and in southern Asia up to the Himalayas.

Species cultivated

P. alba, white poplar, abele, reaching 80ft (24.4m) in cultivation but in poor conditions much smaller, trunks smooth and whitish-grey, young shoots and buds covered with thick grey down; leaves palmately lobed and coarsely toothed, dark green above, white with thick down below, central and southern Europe to western Siberia, naturalised in North America; 'Pyramidalis' (syn. *P. alba* 'Bolleana'), is a columnar cultivar. *P. X serotina*, black Italian poplar, a large tree to

2

1 Populus nigra 'Italica' is a quick-growing narrow fastigiate form of the Lombardy poplar.
2 Platanus X hispanica, the London plane.
3 The multi-coloured bark of the London plane flakes off the trunk in patches.

3

26

130ft (39.6m), often sloping from the prevailing wind, with a wide-spreading, sparsely branched crown; very decorative from the abundance of red female catkins appearing before the leaves, which are copper-coloured and open late in the season, frequently planted. *P. nigra*, black poplar, often exceptionally large tree with heavy limbs, the lower ones arching distinctively downward, when old with large burrs on the trunk, the native British form having downy young shoots and usually found as a male on account of the decorative red catkins, Europe. *P. italica*, Lombardy poplar, distinctive, narrow, spire-like tree occasionally reaching 100ft (30.4m) in cultivation, usually male. *P. tremula*, aspen, 50 to 6oft (15.2 to 18.3m), rarely a large tree, young shoots without down, leaves more or less round with blunt-pointed teeth, hanging on long, flattened stalks which cause them to rustle with the slightest breeze, long catkins produced in late winter, Europe (including Britain) eastwards to Asia Minor and the Caucasus. *P. trichocarpa*, balsam poplar or black cottonwood, usually a tall, pyramidal tree, to 200ft (60.9m), the bark on young trees peeling, the buds sticky and with balsam-like fragrance when breaking, the leaves dark-green above, grey-green below with a prominent mesh-work of fine veins, unfortunately subject to canker, western North America. Other species and hybrids are listed by specialist nurserymen.

Cultivation

Poplars need an open situation in which they must be widely spaced, and fertile, moist soil. Under these conditions they grow rapidly, giving timber that is used for matches and chip baskets for fruit. Planting is carried out in suitable weather at any time during winter. For screening purposes trees are planted 4–6ft (1.2 to 1.8m) apart. However, because of the rate at which their far-ranging roots extract water from the soil it is unwise, where they are grown on clay soils, to plant them closer than 120ft (36.6m) from buildings or walls. On lighter soils the recommended distance is 6oft (18.3m) from walls or buildings. Propagation is easily effected by means of cuttings of dormant wood; commercially, stout stakes (setts) are used.

Prunus

An ancient Latin name (*Rosaceae*). A genus of about 430 species of deciduous or evergreen trees or shrubs, mostly growing in the temperate zone but a few in the Andes of South America. The fruit is a drupe, i.e. a fleshy (often edible) body with a 'skin', the seed within a solitary 'stone'. It includes almonds, apricots, cherries, peaches, plums and nectarines, as well as other purely ornamental species such as cherry-laurel, bird-cherry and Portugal laurel.

Prunus triloba 'Multiplex', the flowering almond, has double or semi-double blooms.

Species cultivated

P. 'Accolade', small floriferous tree with semi-double pink flowers in early spring, hybrid. *P. X amygdalo-persica* 'Pollardii' (D), Pollard's almond, a hybrid between almond and peach, similar to the common almond but with larger richer pink flowers. *P. dulcis* (syn. *P. amygdalus*) (D), almond, 10 to 2oft (3 to 6m), pink flowers in late winter, western Asia; cultivars 'Alba', single white flowers; 'Praecox', flowers pale pink, opening two weeks earlier; 'Roseoplena', flowers pale pink, double. *P. avium* (D), gean, mazzard, or wild cherry, sometimes reaching 6oft (18.3m), flowers white in late spring, leaves colouring brilliantly in autumn, parent of many dessert cherries, Europe, Asia; cultivar 'Plena', with double white flowers, is of great beauty but does not bear fruit. *P. X blireiana* (D), shrub or small tree with purplish leaves and double pink flowers in late winter, hybrid origin. *P. cerasifera* (D), myrobalan or cherry plum, white flowers in early spring, edible yellow or red fruit, western Asia and Caucasus; cultivars 'Pissardi' ('Atropurpurea'), purple-leaf plum, has crimson-purple foliage; both kinds are useful for hedges; *P. cerasus* (D), sour cherry, a small tree with white flowers, one parent of the morello, seldom grown except in the double-flowered

cultivar 'Rhexii', native of western Asia, south-eastern Europe. *P. conradinae* (D), a small, graceful cherry with scented white or pinkish flowers in late winter, central China. *P. X hillieri* (D), broad-crowned tree to 3oft (9.1m), with soft pink flowers and good autumn colour, hybrid origin; 'Spire' is a valuable erect-growing cultivar to 25ft (7.6m). *P. incisa* (D), Fuji cherry, small tree or large shrub, very floriferous in early spring with pinkish buds opening white, Japan. *P. mume* (D), Japanese apricot, small tree, flowers pale pink, late winter to spring, Korea, China; cultivars 'Alba', flowers white; 'Alboplena', flowers double, white, winter and spring. *P.* 'Okame' (D), small tree with carmine-rose flowers in spring, hybrid origin. *P. padus* (D), bird cherry, small tree with white flowers in spikes, spring, fruits black, bitter, Europe (including British Isles), northern Asia to Korea and Japan; cultivars include 'Watereri', with longer flower-spikes. *P. X* 'Pandora' (D), early-flowering small tree with soft pink flowers, hybrid origin. *P. persica* (D), peach, China; ornamental kinds include 'Clara Meyer', double pink; 'Iceberg', white; 'Russell's Red', double crimson; 'Windle Weeping', double pink. *P. sargentii* (D), round-headed, moderate-sized tree with pink flowers in spring with the unfolding red leaves which become fiery red in early autumn, hybrid, native of Japan. *P. serrula* (D), small tree with insignificant flowers but remarkable peeling copper-like bark, native of western China. *P. serrulata* (D), small tree, flowers white, flushed pink, to 2in (50.8mm) across, spring, China, Japan, probably one of the ancestors of some of the 'Japanese' cherries. *P. subhirtella* (D), spring cherry, low-branching tree with very numerous clusters of small flowers pink in bud, opening white, from spring onwards before the leaves open, Japan; cultivars include 'Autumnalis', semi-double flowers from winter onwards; 'Fukubana' has semi-double, deep pink flowers in spring; 'Pendula', pale-pink flowers on slender, weeping branches in spring. *P. triloba* (D), small tree or shrub, to 12ft (3.6m), flowers pinkish, early spring, China; cultivar 'Multiplex', a dwarf flowering almond, bush bearing numerous small, rosette-like double pink flowers along slender branches, early spring. *P. X yedoensis* (D), Yoshino cherry, moderate-sized tree with arching branches bearing almond-scented, single pink flowers in early spring, Japan.

Japanese Cherries

Cherries of obscure origin have been grown in Japan from ancient times. During the present century they have been planted in temperate regions in large numbers. Their attraction is primarily their mass of flowers in spring; few give autumn leaf colour. The flowering season is spring. All are cultivars grown under Japanese names. The best known are: 'Amanogawa', like a dwarf Lombardy poplar, scented, soft-pink double flowers; 'Fugenzo' ('James H. Veitch'), broad-crowned small tree, flowers double, deep pink, late in the season; 'Hisakura', single rose-pink flowers in mid-season; 'Hokusai', flowers early, large double, pale pink; 'Kanzan' ('Sekiyama'), vigorous with erect branches, floriferous with long-stalked, double deep-pink flowers, very popular, mid-season. 'Kiku Shidare Zakura' (Cheal's weeping cherry), a small weeping tree with double pink flowers, mid-season; 'Shirofugen' ('Alborosea'), strong grower, flowers double, pink in bud changing to white, opening late with bronze young leaves; 'Tai-haku', very large white flowers opening among copper-red young leaves which colour yellow in autumn, early to mid-season; 'Ukon', vigorous, flowers palest yellow, somewhat doubled, young leaves copper, mid-season. Others are listed by specialist nurserymen.

Cultivation

All need open, sunny positions in well-drained fertile soil, and do well on lime. Plant during winter. Most dislike pruning, which should be done only during the summer to avoid fungal infection, often fatal to established trees. *P. laurocerasus* and *P. lusitanicus* make excellent evergreen hedges or screens. *P. triloba* 'Multiplex' is sometimes grown in pots for conservatory or cold greenhouse

decoration, using a mixture of 2 parts of sandy loam, 1 part of leafmould, 1 part of sharp sand. The pots are plunged out of doors in summer and brought inside in winter and the plants repotted. Prune them hard after flowering to encourage the production of new flowering shoots. The species can be propagated by seed, or, like the cultivars, budded or grafted on to stocks, *P. cerasifera* or *P. dulcis* forms for plums, damsons and peaches, *P. avium* for cherries. The laurels are reproduced by cuttings taken in mid-summer or by seed. A number with thin stems, including *P. subhirtella* and its cultivars, can be layered.

Pyrus

The ancient Latin name for a pear tree (*Rosaceae*). Pear. A genus of about 30 species of deciduous trees with flowers borne in clusters, usually white, followed by edible fruit (pyriform in shape) containing gritty cells embedded in the flesh; this is a characteristic of the genus. It is widely distributed in Europe, eastern Asia, North Africa, Persia and Russia. The genus formerly included whitebeams, rowans and apples, which are now included under *Sorbus* and *Malus*, respectively.

Species cultivated

P. salicifolia 'Pendula', willow-leaved pear, 15 to 25ft (4.5 to 7.6m), graceful, weeping habit, narrow, silvery leaves, flowers white to cream, spring, fruits brown, south-eastern Europe, Asia Minor. *P. ussuriensis*, snow pear, to 40ft (12.2m) in its native habitat, flowers white, 1 to 1½in (25.4 to 38.1mm) across, borne in dense clusters, fruits yellowish-green, leaves bronzy-red in autumn, north-eastern Asia.

Cultivation

These hardy trees will grow in most soils and situations, doing best in a sunny one. Plant in late autumn and winter, and prune in winter to keep the shape if required. Propagation is from seed stratified over winter and sown ½in (12.7mm) deep out of doors in early spring, or by grafting on to wild pear stock in early spring.

Quercus

The ancient Latin name of an oak tree (*Fagaceae*). Oak. A genus of some 450 species of deciduous or evergreen trees and a small number of shrubs distributed over the temperate regions of the northern hemisphere and on high mountains in parts of South America and Asia. The pollen-bearing flowers are in catkins, the minute females developing in one or two years into the distinctive acorn (botanically a nut), in a cup from which it parts when ripe, often to be distributed by birds or beasts dropping it by accident when carrying it

away for food. Many species are of noble proportions and the timber is of great economic value. The leaves of many deciduous kinds colour well in autumn.

Species cultivated

Q. borealis (syn. *Q. rubra*) (D), red oak, reaching 100ft (30.4m) or more in cultivation, bark grey, smooth except in old trees, deciduous, leaves broad with few deep lobes ending in bristle-like tip, turning brown or red in autumn, acorns broad-based in shallow cups on short stalk, ripening in second year. *Q. cerrid*, Turkey oak, large erect tree to 120ft (36.6m), bark furrowed, winter buds distinctively surrounded by long, narrow scales, leaves very deeply and irregularly lobed, acorns up to 1in (25.4mm) long, ripening in second year, Europe and western Asia, sometimes naturalised in British Isles; *Q. coccinea* (D), scarlet oak, to 80ft (24.4m) in cultivation, bark grey and smooth until old age, leaves long-stalked, deeply cut, much more so than *Q. borealis*, into up to 7 lobes, bristle-tipped, turning scarlet in autumn, acorns (not freely produced) up to 1in (25.4mm) long, eastern North America. *Q. cerrid*, leaves leathery, long stalked, up to 3in (76.2mm) long, toothed, falling in mid-summer, acorns up to 1in (25.4mm) long, a natural hybrid, plants raised from acorns vary considerably, *Q. ilex* (E), evergreen or holm oak, round-headed tree, variable in size, bark dark grey divided into small scales, shoots downy, leaves leathery, variable, either entire or somewhat toothed, to 3½in (88.9mm) long, acorns about 1in (25.4mm) long, southern Europe, withstands seashore conditions. *Q. palustris* (D), pin oak, a graceful tree to 80ft (24.4m) in cultivation, the slender branches distinctively drooping then up-turning at their ends, leaves long-stalked, the blades up to 6in (152mm) long with 5 to 7 deeply cut lobes, colouring well in autumn, acorns (infrequently borne) ½in (12.7mm) long, eastern United States. *Q. petraea* (syn. *Q. sessiliflora*), sessile or Durmast oak, massive deciduous tree reaching 120ft (36.6m) in cultivation, with rounded head and fairly straight branches, leaves downy below with star-shaped hairs, lobing variable, acorns almost stalkless, one of the two common oaks in the British Isles, native of Europe and western Asia; cultivars 'Purpurea' (syn. 'Rubicunda'), young leaves reddish-purple, flushed red when older. *Q. phellos* (D), willow oak, to 100ft (30.4m) in nature, less tall in cultivation, often columnar in habit, leaves narrow, to 5in (127mm) long, colouring well in autumn, acorns small, North America. *Q. robur* (D), English or pedunculate oak, massive round-headed tree with crooked branches, reaching 120ft (36.6m) in cultivation, leaves very short stalked with ear-like projections on either side of their base, down on the underside sparse and consisting of straight hairs, acorns on long stalks, the other common oak

1 *Pyrus salicifolia 'Pendula', the willow-leaved pear, is a graceful weeping tree with silvery leaves and white flowers.*
2 *Quercus robur (syn. Q. pedunculata) is the common oak, with a fine head of stout branches and attractive tracery in winter and early spring. A traditional feature of the English country scene.*

of the British Isles, Europe, North Africa and western Asia; cultivars 'Cristata', leaves curled; 'Fastigiata', habit columnar; 'Filicifolia' leaves divided into narrow segments. *Q. suber* (E), cork oak, tree with rounded head reaching 70ft (21.3m) in mild districts, bark silvery-grey, thick and rough, providing cork, the twigs very downy, leaves long-stalked, leathery, dark green above, grey with felted down below, usually with a few shallow teeth on the margin, the blades up to 2½in (63.5mm) long, acorns up to 1in (25.4mm) long, southern Europe, North Africa, does best in the warmer areas of the temperate region.

Cultivation

All oaks thrive in deep, fertile soil, and are very wind-firm. They do not tolerate shade. Plant deciduous kinds in autumn or spring, evergreen kinds autumn or early spring. Any necessary pruning of evergreen kinds should be done in early spring, of deciduous kinds in mid-winter. Most of those named above are very hardy except *Q. suber* which will only flourish in mild districts. Propagation is by the acorns, which must be sown at once on ripening as they lose their fertility on drying. The seedlings should be planted out in their permanent positions as soon as they are large enough, to allow the vigorous tap-root to develop. Cultivars must be grafted or budded on common oak.

Salix

The old Latin name (*Salicaceae*). Willow. Deciduous, rarely evergreen, trees and shrubs with narrow, alternate, rarely opposite, leaves. The male and female flowers are on separate trees in the form of catkins, the male being showy with yellow pollen, and the female remaining green. The seed is wind blown on a tuft of down. There are some 300 species or, according to some botanists, about 500 (the species are notoriously difficult to classify), found principally in cool and temperate regions of the northern hemisphere. They make attractive specimen trees, and are particularly useful in that they will grow in wet and badly drained situations. They are also of use commercially, for basket work and cricket bats.

Species cultivated

S. acutifolia (syn. *S. daphnoides acutifolia*), small tree, graceful in habit, shoots slender, violet-purple with white bloom, catkins showy, Russia, Turkestan. *S. alba*, white willow, Huntingdon willow, large erect tree to 70 to 80ft (21.3 to 24.4m), of narrow outline unless pollarded, narrow leaves covered with silvery hair, Europe, Asia; cultivars 'Aurea', branches golden-yellow, leaves pale yellow; 'Chermesina' ('Britzensis'), young shoots brilliant orange-scarlet; 'Tristis' see *X chrysocoma* 'Vitellina', golden willow, smaller than the species with rich yellow young shoots. *S. X chrysocoma* (syn. *S.a.* 'Tristis'), the commonest large weeping willow, the shoots yellow in winter and bearing both male and female flowers on the same tree. *S. caprea*, palm or goat willow, sallow, tall shrub or small tree, 10 to 25ft (3 to 7.6m), leaves broad and pointed, the golden male, and silvery-green female, catkins appearing before the leaves in early spring, are of great beauty, Europe, including Britain, Asia. *S. X caerulea*, cricket bat willow, 70 to 100ft (21.3 to 30.4m), fast growing, pyramidal in habit, similar to *S. alba*, but the female form only is known, Britain. *S. daphnoides*, violet willow, distinctive small tree with purplish shoots having a silvery bloom, male and female catkins appearing before the leaves in early spring are very attractive, Europe (not British Isles), central Asia. *S. fragilis*, crack willow, a large spreading tree 90 to 100ft (27.4 to 30.4m), with narrow leaves and slender twigs which snap off when bent, often planted where the fine root system will stabilise the banks of pools, canals, and so on, native of Europe (including British Isles), western Asia. *S. matsudana*, tree to 40ft (12.2m), with yellowish-green shoots and narrow leaves, usually grown as the cultivar 'Tortuosa', with branches and twigs much twisted, northern China, Manchuria and Korea. *S. pentandra*, bay willow, shrub or small tree, to 30ft (9.1m), young shoots lustrous, brownish-green, sticky, leaves elliptic, lustrous green above, large golden catkins on leafy stalks, late spring, Europe (including British Isles) to Caucasus.

S. purpurea, purple osier, shrub or tree to 10ft (3m) or more, shoots slender, purplish, catkins to 1in (25.4mm) long, Europe, including Britain, central Asia. *S. viminalis*, common osier, shrub or tree to 20ft (6m) or more, leaves narrow to 10ins (254mm) long, silvery below, catkins to 1¼in (31.7mm) long, spring, Europe (including Britain).

Cultivation

The willows are easily grown trees or shrubs, most of them requiring a permanently moist soil on the heavy side; they do not object to periodical flooding. Plant in autumn or winter, and prune to shape if required in winter also. Pollarding should be carried out in late winter. Where the colour of the bark of young shoots is a feature, cut back hard in early spring each year. Propagate from cuttings of any age or size during autumn or winter driven firmly into moist soil. Choice varieties can be budded in mid-summer, or grafted at the beginning of spring. The dwarf kinds are suitable for the rock garden, the smallest kinds for trough and sink gardens, in almost any kind of soil. They make handsome specimen plants for shallow plant containers.

Tilia

The ancient Latin name for the lime (*Tiliaceae*). Lime, linden; in North America whitewoods and basswoods. There are about 50 species found in the temperate regions of the northern hemisphere, in North America south to Mexico (but none in western North America), and in parts of China and Japan. All are deciduous, with alternate leaves, more or less heart-shaped and are long-lived trees, reaching on average, 800 to 1,000 years. The small, green-white or yellowish, scented flowers are borne in drooping clusters subtended by a winged bract, having five sepals and five petals; they open at about midsummer and produce nectar freely. The small fruits are nut-like. The smooth bark of some species can be detached in long strips, the fibres being used for weaving and tying. The white timber is finely grained and is used for interior work, such as wood carving. Some kinds become badly attacked by aphids.

Species cultivated

T. americana, basswood or American lime, a large tree to 130ft (39.6m) in the wild, the leaves sometimes 9in (229mm) long. *T.*

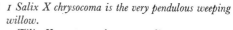

1 Salix X chrysocoma is the very pendulous weeping willow.
2 Tilia X europaea, the common lime.

cordata (syn. *T. parvifolia*), small-leaved lime, a slow-growing tree eventually reaching 100ft (30.4m), distinguished by the spreading, not pendent position of the inflorescence, Europe (including Britain). *T. X europaea* (syn. *T. vulgaris*), linden, lime, hybrid between *T. platyphyllos* and *T. cordata*, very commonly planted but sometimes considered to be unsightly because of bushy growths on the trunk, either parent being preferable. *T. petiolaris*, weeping silver lime, widely spreading tree to 50ft (15.2m), of handsome form with large leaves silvery on the undersides, flowers very sweetly scented, their abundant nectar often stupifies bees, probably from south-eastern Europe. *T. platyphyllos*, (syn. *T. grandifolia*), large-leaved lime a rare native of Britain, a fine, quick-growing large tree to 100ft (30.4m), Europe. *T. tomentosa*, silver lime, tree to 60ft (18.3m), leaves drawn out into a long point, sometimes slightly lobed at the base, with white down on the underside, south-eastern Europe.

Cultivation

Limes will thrive on any reasonably good soil, doing well on quite shallow, limestone soils, and can be planted during late autumn and winter. They stand pruning, and were formerly much used for pleaching – the interweaving of the branches of closely planted trees, subsequently pruned to form an espalier-like, tall hedge. Propagation is best from seed, which often does not germinate until the second spring after sowing. Layering is also practised.

Ulmus procera 'Vanhouttei' is an attractive golden-leaved form of the magnificent common English hedgerow elm.

Ulmus

The ancient Latin name (*Ulmaceae*). Elm. A genus of 45 species, widely distributed in the temperate areas of the northern hemisphere, Indo-China and Mexico, consisting mostly of deciduous trees. The leaves are alternate, usually asymmetrical at the base, and toothed. In most species small flowers with prominent red anthers appear before the leaves open in spring, and are followed quickly by the green, disc-like winged fruits. Most produce suckers freely. On many kinds corky shoots are found.

Species cultivated

U. americana, white elm, to 130ft (39.6m), limbs spreading outwards, branchlets pendulous; much planted in its native North America on account of its handsome form but seldom growing satisfactorily in Britain. *U. carpinifolia* (syn. *U. nitens*), suckering tree to 100ft (30.4m) outer branches pendulous, twigs smooth, leaves small, very unequal at the base, without hairs, glossy on the upper surface; a good windbreak, Europe, western Asia; cultivars 'Cornubiensis', Cornish elm, has a compact crown formed from few heavy limbs; a distinctive tree seldom seen outside Cornwall and Devon; *U. sarniensis*, the Wheatley, Jersey or Guernsey elm, tall tree of narrow, flame-like form frequently planted in streets and avenues, often mistaken for the Cornish elm, but having a much finer branching system; *sarniensis* 'Aurea' (syn. 'Dicksonii'), Dickson's golden elm, slow-growing form with golden leaves. *U. glabra* (syn. *U. montana*), wych or Scotch elm, 100 to 125ft (30.4 to 28.1m), one of the most majestic native trees, particularly in the north, able to withstand gales and severe weather, crown broad, branchlets somewhat pendulous, young shoots downy, leaves very unequal at the base, with rough hairs on the upper surface, sometimes they are three-lobed at the apex, northern Europe (including Britain); cultivars 'Camperdownii' has a rounded head of very pendulous branches; 'Exoniensis' (*fastigiata*), small, erect-growing tree, leaves and twigs often twisted; 'Lutescens', leaves pale yellow; 'Pendula', broad crown of spreading, somewhat weeping branches from which the branchlets hang. *U. X hollandica* 'Belgica', Belgian elm, vigorous tree resembling the wych elm; *U. X h.* 'Major', of the same parentage, the so-called Dutch elm though not coming from Holland, to 120ft (36.6m), with a short, broad, trunk and a wide-spreading crown, branches pendulous at their ends, shoots often corky, suckering freely. *U. procera* (syn. *U. campestris*), English hedgerow elm, a majestic, sparsely branched, erect tree from 100 to 150ft (30.4 to 45.7m), found in the hedgerows and avenues of England, it does not produce fertile seed and increases by means of suckers, leaves very unequal at the base, rough on the upper surface; cultivars 'Argenteovariegata', leaves marked attractively with creamy-white; 'Vanhouttei', handsome golden leaves. *U. X vegeta* (*U. carpinifolia X U. glabra*), Huntingdon or Chichester elm, suckering tree to 100ft (30.4m), upward, ascending branches, leaves 5 to 6in (127 to 152mm) long.

Cultivation

Elms will thrive in a wide range of soils, are extremely hardy and will withstand strong wind. They are subject to the disease known as Dutch elm disease, a fungus disease spread by a beetle which burrows under the bark. The shoots lose their leaves prematurely and develop a distorted shape like a shepherd's crook. Later, the branch and ultimately the entire tree may die. Large, dead branches may be removed as sometimes trees recover. Dead wood should not be left lying on the ground but burned as the beetles will breed in it. The wych elm (*U. glabra*) is probably most affected. The hedgerow elm (*U. procera*) has a tendency to drop apparently healthy limbs unexpectedly on calm summer days. Though this is not a very common happening, it is as well not to plant this valuable tree where the branches will overhang a public way. Propagation of those kinds that produce suckers is by detaching these with as much root as possible in winter. Seed, sown as soon as ripe, can be used for the others.

SHRUBS

basic planning

The virtues of a shrub garden are many, for shrubs come in all shapes and sizes, deciduous and evergreen. Most flower, a lot berry too — and combined with permutations of leaf colour and texture with stem interest as well, the variety is endless. For the modern garden owner who is looking for ways of providing height, colour and beauty for a minimum maintenance effort, shrubs can be the perfect answer.

But shrubs must be carefully chosen and skilfully used — and before you start, it is essential to know the eventual height, shape, flowering season, foliage colour and hardiness of a suitable range of shrubs. Soil and site must be taken into consideration and the temperatures and weather conditions of where you live. This book breaks down the information into relevant headings and listings for all requirements. 150 selected shrubs are illustrated and described in detail, with supplementary lists of shrubs showing the main characteristics of each group. If you find that you like the look of a certain shrub but the particular variety is not available in your area, check with your local nursery — chances are they may have a similar variety.

In addition there are several garden plans and elevations to help you visualize the sort of effect that can be obtained. As the framework of a garden, collections of shrubs are invaluable used in shrubberies, beds or borders. You can also use many aromatic shrubs, especially herby plants like rosemary, sage, lavender and even some of the thymes, at the edge of a terrace where their fragrance

Carefully chosen, shrubs can provide a variety of effects with contrasting foliage colour.

can be appreciated or in the more relaxed layout of the informal garden. So, before you get carried away with the beautiful blossoms of a magnolia or the purple foliage of *Prunus* 'Cistina', first consider the overall effect you want to create. Then draw up a list of the basic qualities of the site, taking into account the various likes and dislikes of shrubs.

Landscaping with shrubs

How then to select when building up a collection from scratch? First arm yourself with a good catalogue from your local supplier, preferably a nursery or garden centre, and make a drawing to scale of the area which you propose to plant. Shrubs will be with you for a long time, so it is well worth some initial homework before selecting them. Visit a local park, a garden open to the public or even a garden centre to see the different types thriving in your area.

Evergreens for background

Start by considering the background shrubs. Their back-up job will be far better if they are evergreen, as they will then be effective through the winter too. These background shrubs are a staple factor in the whole of your garden layout. In fact, they create the bones of it, as well as providing a screen for shelter or privacy. Your catalogue should tell you the height and breadth of the shrub in a given number of years. Compose your border by drawing in individual shrubs to scale.

Middle height and foreground

Come down in size now, still thinking in evergreen (or evergrey) terms, and select middle height and foreground shrubs. As well as considering dimensions, make a choice based on leaf colour and overall shape for contrast. (Flower colour is usually of secondary importance when used with evergreens, but think of this too, sticking to a particular colour range.)
The first evergreen selection should provide interest throughout the year and, if properly selected, some useful winter foliage and flowers for the house.

Deciduous shrubs

Repeat the process now, thinking in terms of deciduous shrubs. Consider the large ones first, even planting slower-growing evergreens between them, but allow plenty of room for all to develop fully. Work your way from the back of the border to the front. Colour will play important an part, so keep to a specific range.

Spacing

The beginner tends to plant too many things too close together in a border. So, having checked that everything will grow in your particular conditions it is safe to say you can leave out about half of the plants you had first envisaged. The object is to create a bold, simple composition of shrubs the way a flower arranger might compose a bowl of flowers. You will never fit all the varieties you want into one bed, so settle for three or four plants of one type, and contrast them with another group of similar size (more, of course, if the bed is large). The result will be much more positive than a random selection of one of this and one of that. Use plants of strong character sparsely. They become sculptural features within the layout and, if used too liberally, they unsettle the composition.

planning a garden

Not only the nature of the plot and its particular problems but the style of a house, too, should influence your choice of plants, paving and garden furniture—and a garden should be planned as carefully as the inside of a house where one tries to achieve some sort of co-ordination.

In this first section on garden planning, landscape designer John Brookes shows step by step how he sets about planning a particular garden for a particular client and making the functional requirements an integral part of the design. This is followed by a section on how to draw up your own plan.

Then come four more garden plans which deal with specific problems: A. the hot sunny corner; B. the front garden; C. the shady garden with large existing tree; D. the garden with an odd shape.

Do not be put off by the geometric appearance of the garden plans. Remember, plants grow into very undiciplined shapes and a neat, orderly design is called for—when the plants grow up and out the final result will be far from stiff and formal.

The site

The site is flat and featureless, 30' by 25' (9.1 by 7.6m), part of a new suburban development, with a house on the left and another house, some distance away, from the right hand end of the garden. The right hand side of the garden is partly masked by the garage.

The owners' wants

The clients were open minded about the design of the garden, but wanted it to allow for the following:
1. A compost or bonfire area (this area would be equally suitable for vegetables or a children's sandpit).
2. A greenhouse and frame area.
Both areas 1 and 2 should be screened from the house as far as possible.
3. A good sitting and sunbathing area which would also serve as a main play area for the children.
The remainder to be decorative, but maintenance free.

A A basic plan of the garden is drawn up following the steps under 'How to draw a plan'.
Areas 1, 2 and 3 are sketched in bearing in mind the direction of the sun.

B Areas for shrub planting are marked in roughly to provide screens from the house to the left and at the far end of the garden, to provide a low screen for the compost and bonfire

area, and to make a focal point in the middle distance.

C The next step is to visualize roughly how the flat plan will look in 3-D from the sitting room, to make sure the balance works, that a long view is maintained, that features needed to be blocked out are coped with. Most important, it is necessary to see—particularly with shrubs—that a good three dimensional effect is created, with foreground, middle distance and background, just as though it were a stage set. John Brookes adds a small tree in the middle distance which acts as a visual pivot around which the design sweeps, and which contrasts with the verticals of the conifers at the back right, sited to screen the neighbour's house. He also suggests reducing the level of the foreground area, which is to be paved, by taking away the topsoil—this will provide an interesting change of level and relieve the flatness of the site.

D If you find it difficult to make a perspective drawing, you will find it much simpler to make a rough scale model, cutting out chunks of card to scale, and moving them about like model soldiers or scenery in a toy theatre until you get the result you want. Get down and peer along the plan from the 'sitting room window' level, then move things about until the composition looks good, and the screening is effective.

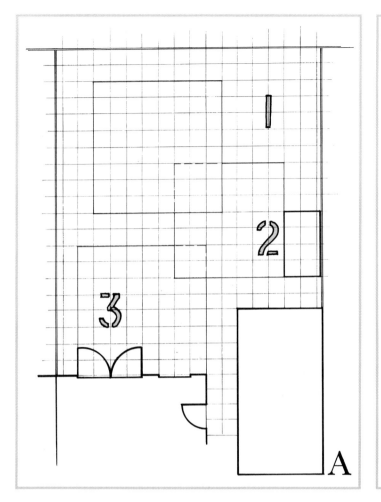

A

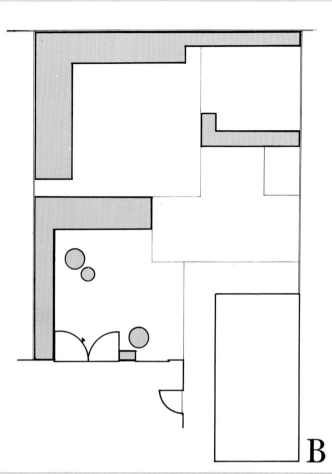

B

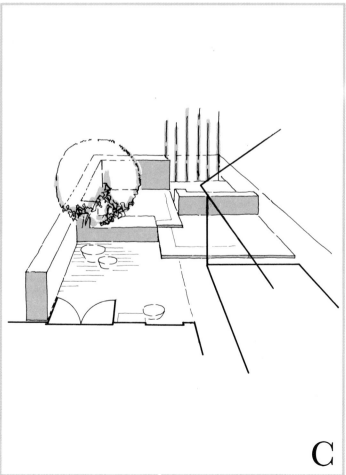

C

This is a cardboard model of the client's site. Coloured card was used to make the trees, plants and lawn areas. Cut out the plants to the required shape with a rectangular tab at the foot of plant to attach it to the base. To make the plants and base firm, stick two layers of card together. Bend the tab at right angles to the plant then stick tab to base. The size of the base should be the eventual girth of the plant—this way you can determine how close together the plants should be.

D

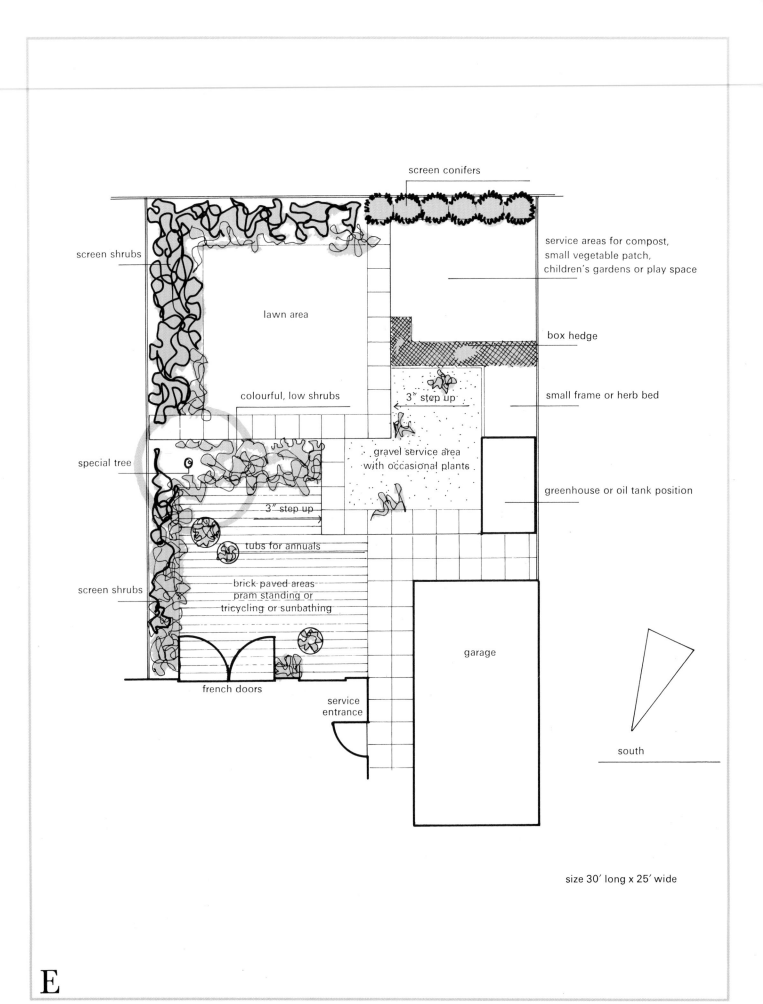

screen conifers

screen shrubs

service areas for compost,
small vegetable patch,
children's gardens or play space

lawn area

box hedge

colourful, low shrubs

3" step up

small frame or herb bed

gravel service area
with occasional plants

special tree

3" step up

greenhouse or oil tank position

tubs for annuals

brick paved areas
pram standing or
tricycling or sunbathing

screen shrubs

french doors

garage

service
entrance

south

size 30' long x 25' wide

E The final layout is a simple work-
   able pattern, applicable to many
situations and average family requirements. Decisions have yet to be made as
to the types of infill—paving or gravel,
grass or ground cover, shrubs or annuals.
Much will depend on prices and time
available for maintenance. The style
of the house, too, will influence the
choice of material, and later the pots
you use and the garden seating.
A period Victorian house might have a
slightly fussy garden, with Victorian urns
and metal furniture; and the paving
could be crazy, or tiles for a sheltered
situation.
A modern garden would have bolder,
cleaner lines and plain containers stand
about, containing bright annual colour.
Plain concrete slabs have been used to
emphasize the garden pattern, which is
of interlocking squares. Brick is used
in the terrace area near the house.
Gravel is used in another area, making
the transition from the hard brick surface
to the lawn of the top square. The
service/play areas could be grass or
consolidated gravel.

F Now choose the skeleton or background plants.
Trees first: six *Cupressocyparis Leylandii*
will block the view at the back. A
Eucalyptus gunii makes a feature in the
middle distance—this acts as a sort of
pivot around which the design works.
Shrubs next: choose the plants which
will shelter your garden, provide privacy
throughout the year and generally
provide a background to the other, more
flowery shrubs to be chosen later.
Select a good proportion of evergreens
to provide year-round interest. There
are many to choose from some with
colour or variegated foliage, berries and
flowers.
As many evergreen shrubs grow slower
than many deciduous shrubs, interplant
them with quick growing shrubs, such as
buddleia and broom, which can ultimately be taken out.
Choose the internal divisions—in this
particular case a hedge of box (*Buxus
sempervirens* 'Handsworthensis').
Broadly shrubs have been chosen to contrast with the grey of the eucalyptus,
such as the blue ceanothus.

G The infill plants bring the garden
   to life. These should be considered
as one so that the completed garden is
not a spotty series of incidents.
The colour arrangement has been worked
round the eucalyptus—a purple vine on
the fence behind it, grey santolina,
white floribunda roses with silvery pink
cistus nearby.
Shrub height is important. Here the

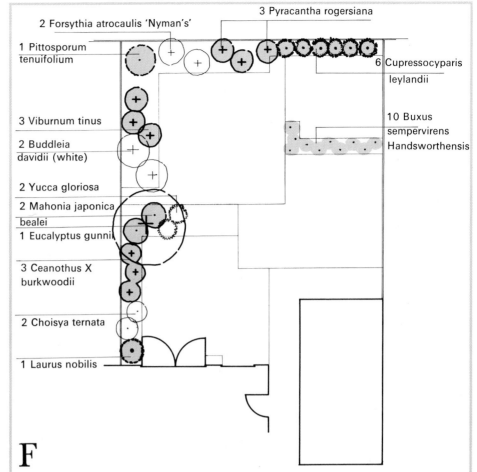

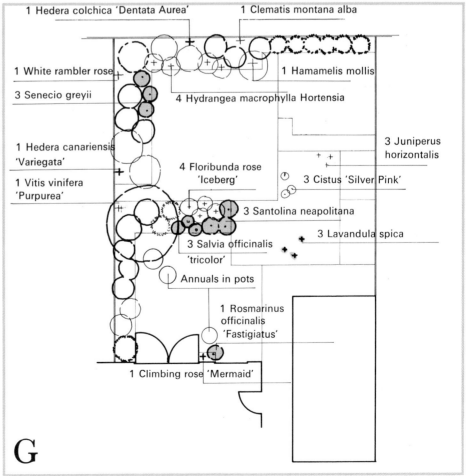

shrubs in the bed across the centre of the garden—the middle distance—will sweep down from the eucalyptus into the middle. Form, too, has been considered, and spiky yuccas are contrasted with bold mahonia leaves for instance.

Adjacent to the house on the hot, sunny wall, and around the terrace, plant shrubs with scented foliage of flowers. Here the choice is rosemary and bay.

Lastly, why not climbers up the house? The choice here is the semi-evergreen rose Mermaid. Think carefully before using ivy as birds tend to nest in it. Also if yours is a very old house with soft mortar between the bricks, the aerial roots of ivy or climbing hydrangea can creep between.

H The garden as the hopeful mind's eye visualizes it in 3 to 4 years! Of course, not everything will be flowering at once, but many of the shrubs will have filled out nicely, the eucalyptus will have grown tall, shimmery and light foliaged—the screen of cypress will be effectively blacking out the neighbour's house, every month will provide new delights by way of flowers, fragrance and leaf colour.

Obviously some thinning of shrubs will be necessary with time. Take out subjects so that others can breathe, especially when two or three have been planted originally. The removal of the odd shrub is far better practice than trying to suppress and prune a shrub to keep in with your original conception.

It should always be remembered that a garden is a growing, moving thing, so that the ultimate picture is never realized. You perhaps achieve a series of pictures, but they will be different each year, as plants grow upwards and outwards at different rates.

38

how to draw a plan

1. Measure up the site, noting down any existing features worth retaining. Take measurements of the boundaries from the house, and at 90 degrees to it (figure I).

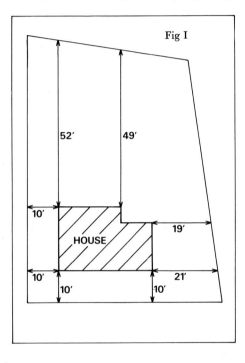

The relation between boundary and house is now established and the house can be used as the base for all measurements to individual objects. To check the exact position of an existing tree, take measurements to it from two corners of the house, so forming a triangle (figure II).

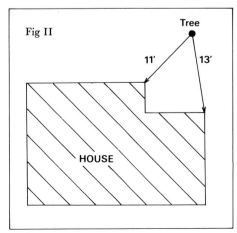

2. Make a scaled down drawing of the site, preferably on graph paper, to a standard scale of ⅛″ to 1′0″ or 1/10″ to 1′0″ (or in metric the nearest similar scales are 1:100 or 1:50). Accurately draw in all features measured so far. To mark in the position of a proposed tree, or any other feature, measure the distance from two corners of the house (AB, figure III). Set a pair of compasses to scale to the distance from A to the tree. Draw an arc from point A. Similarly draw an arc from B using the distance of B from the object. Where the arcs intersect is the position of the tree.

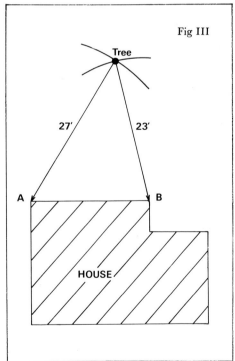

3. Note where South lies, and whether there are any particular views you want to block, or make anything of as a feature.

4. Bearing in mind the position of the sun, site in what seems the obvious position for the terrace area, storage point, rubbish corner, greenhouse, vegetable plot, washing line and play space—all the most convenient positions for the things you want to do in the garden.

5. Evolve a simple pattern which will embrace all the features you have on site (if any) and all the things you want to do in it. Think about pattern only, and forget plants for a while. It could be one of circles, or interlocking squares —get ideas from garden plan books or even modern abstract paintings—for, basically, while an artist fills his canvas with paint, you do the same thing in the garden on a larger scale, using areas of planting, paving and gravel instead.

6. Having evolved a pattern in the abstract, start to rationalise it to a functional working plan. Think about surfacings linking up areas of activity (they need not be straight paths). Think about areas of texture—gravel, grass or ground cover.

7. Having evolved a working plan two dimensionally, start to think about it in 3-D. The painting now becomes a sculpture. Decide on the heights of the masses you have evolved in your plan. These will control the perspective view of the garden from the house, from where you will be aware of your foreground, middle, and far distance. You will also see how important the spaces are between the masses. For too long gardeners have concentrated on the content of the masses alone in their garden plans, so that the over-all effect lacks any form of cohesion.

8. Now start to consider in detail the plant content of those masses, the particular shapes you want in them, their height, and what you ask them to do—to frame a view or hide it, provide shelter or privacy. Let the main masses of your planting reinforce the lines of your plan. This working planting is the skeleton or bones of your garden; it will contain it.

9. Only when you have worked out the skeleton planting should you infill it with the smaller prettier subjects, which are the star attractions.

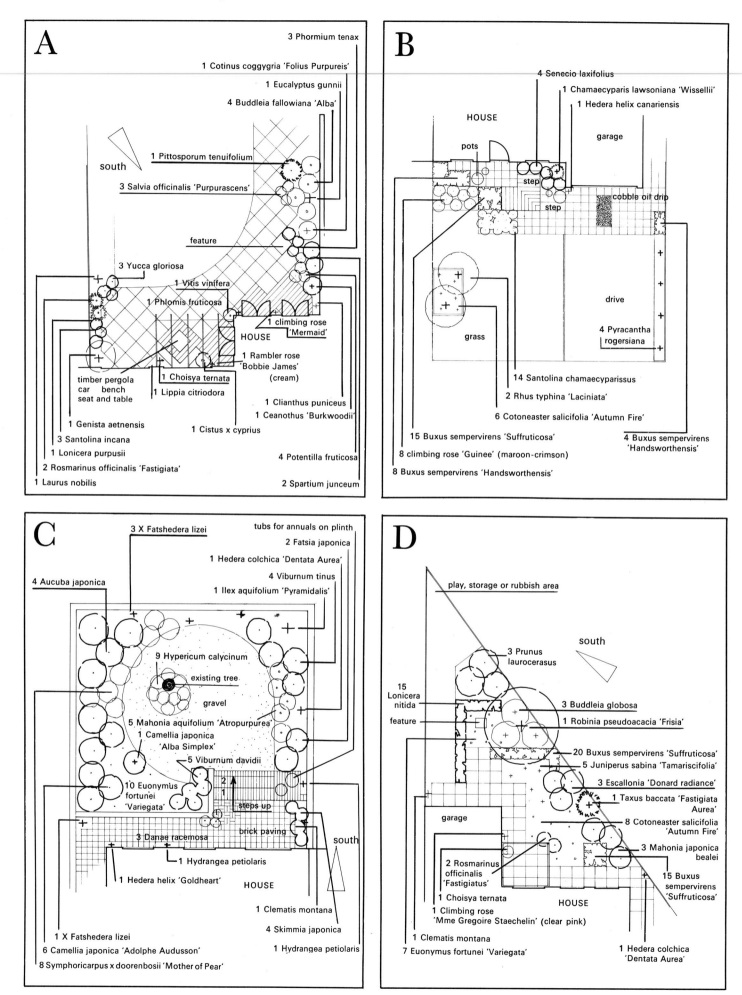

A

3 Phormium tenax
1 Cotinus coggygria 'Folius Purpureis'
1 Eucalyptus gunnii
4 Buddleia fallowiana 'Alba'
1 Pittosporum tenuifolium
south
3 Salvia officinalis 'Purpurascens'
feature
3 Yucca gloriosa
1 Vitis vinifera
1 Phlomis fruticosa
1 climbing rose 'Mermaid'
HOUSE
1 Rambler rose 'Bobbie James' (cream)
timber pergola
car bench
seat and table
1 Choisya ternata
1 Lippia citriodora
1 Clianthus puniceus
1 Ceanothus 'Burkwoodii'
1 Genista aetnensis
1 Cistus x cyprius
3 Santolina incana
1 Lonicera purpusii
2 Rosmarinus officinalis 'Fastigiata'
4 Potentilla fruticosa
1 Laurus nobilis
2 Spartium junceum

B

4 Senecio laxifolius
1 Chamaecyparis lawsoniana 'Wissellii'
1 Hedera helix canariensis
HOUSE
pots
garage
step
step
cobble oil drip
drive
grass
4 Pyracantha rogersiana
14 Santolina chamaecyparissus
2 Rhus typhina 'Laciniata'
6 Cotoneaster salicifolia 'Autumn Fire'
15 Buxus sempervirens 'Suffruticosa'
8 climbing rose 'Guinee' (maroon-crimson)
8 Buxus sempervirens 'Handsworthensis'
4 Buxus sempervirens 'Handsworthensis'

C

3 X Fatshedera lizei
tubs for annuals on plinth
2 Fatsia japonica
1 Hedera colchica 'Dentata Aurea'
4 Viburnum tinus
1 Ilex aquifolium 'Pyramidalis'
4 Aucuba japonica
9 Hypericum calycinum
existing tree
gravel
5 Mahonia aquifolium 'Atropurpurea'
1 Camellia japonica 'Alba Simplex'
5 Viburnum davidii
10 Euonymus fortunei 'Variegata'
steps up
brick paving
3 Danae racemosa
south
1 Hydrangea petiolaris
1 Hedera helix 'Goldheart'
HOUSE
1 Clematis montana
4 Skimmia japonica
1 Hydrangea petiolaris
1 X Fatshedera lizei
6 Camellia japonica 'Adolphe Audusson'
8 Symphoricarpus x doorenbosii 'Mother of Pear'

D

play, storage or rubbish area
south
3 Prunus laurocerasus
15 Lonicera nitida
feature
3 Buddleia globosa
1 Robinia pseudoacacia 'Frisia'
20 Buxus sempervirens 'Suffruticosa'
5 Juniperus sabina 'Tamariscifolia'
3 Escallonia 'Donard radiance'
1 Taxus baccata 'Fastigiata Aurea'
8 Cotoneaster salicifolia 'Autumn Fire'
garage
3 Mahonia japonica bealei
15 Buxus sempervirens 'Suffruticosa'
2 Rosmarinus officinalis 'Fastigiatus'
1 Choisya ternata
HOUSE
1 Climbing rose 'Mme Gregoire Staechelin' (clear pink)
1 Clematis montana
7 Euonymus fortunei 'Variegata'
1 Hedera colchica 'Dentata Aurea'

A The hot sunny corner

A pergola is a most attractive and effective way of providing dappled shade in a sunny area. So, to take advantage of the sunny aspect, the whole corner is treated as a large terrace with a sun room and a pergola along one wall. A pergola basically consists of wooden poles resting on brick or wooden pillars about 6 feet apart and 7½ to 9 feet high (1.8 m apart and 2 to 2.7 m high). Resting across the main poles are cross poles spaced at about 2 foot intervals. These then make an excellent support for all sorts of vines and ramblers, to provide height and foreground interest.

This pergola is covered with a white rambler rose and underneath are a built-in table and bench.

The shrubs round the edges are from those especially suited to hot, sheltered conditions and the chosen colour scheme is in blues, yellows and greys.

B An open front garden

The problems of a front garden are quite different from those of a back garden. It is not the same lived-in affair. Basically the garden needs to look neat from the road and, if possible, it should provide a bit of privacy to the front windows without cutting out the light.

A front garden is not the place to hang out ones washing or for the children's sand pit or for the compost or rubbish. Rather than functional, it is, like the front of the house, on display.

The plan keeps the garden very simple with lawn and paving and a few splashes of colour. Evergreens are used to give privacy to the front window.

Note the cobble oil drip in the paving area to stop unsightly oil patches from the car.

C A shady 'town' garden

This garden has been designed to work round an existing large tree. The main part of the garden is two steps up from the area outside the sitting room. Both the house and the garden walls are in old stock brick which has been used for all the paving and steps.

The most dense area of shadow has largely been filled with gravel.

Although some of the shrubs used, such as the camellia, are renowned for their flowers, the planting is mainly of evergreens, relying largely on foliage shapes and colours for strong effect.

Annuals have been planted in pots by the side of the house not in the shadow of the tree.

For other suitable shubs see the section on shady sites

D A plant lover's garden

Here the awkward deep triangular shape of the garden makes the familiar formula of flat lawn or paved area bordered with fore, middle and background planting unfeasible. One solution, suggested here, is a mass of flower and plant display—which is the plant lover's delight.

This could result in a spotty uncoordinated collection of shrubs. So, to avoid this, John Brookes has made strong use of evergreens to hold the design together.

The shape of the garden has been exploited and the sharp bottom corner screened off to make a storage area, which could equally well be used as a children's play area or for compost or rubbish. Cutting off this corner also helps disguise the awkward shape of the site.

choosing and caring for shrubs

What, exactly, is a shrub?

Unlike herbaceous perennials such as michaelmas daisy and golden rod, the true shrub does not die down to the ground each autumn. Its stems become woody and increase in length year by year, branching to form the structure we recognise as a shrub. When mature its basic form will either be a cluster of several woody stems rising from below ground level, or a short thick trunk branching at or just above the ground. Some shrub species get very large and it is often difficult to draw the line between shrub and tree. However, if the plant has the above characteristics, and is less than 10 to 15ft (3 to 4.5m) in height, it can be considered a shrub. Above this height it should be called a tree, even though the true tree form has a single stem or trunk rising 4 to 6ft (1.2 to 1.8m) above ground level before the first branch.

Soil

The average shrub is easy to please if certain basic factors are taken into consideration. Firstly the soil must be fertile and reasonably well-drained. Most garden soil benefits from a dressing of organic material such as decayed manure or compost, leaf-mould or peat, plus a general fertilizer.

The basic soil types are clay, sand and loam.

Clay. A clay soil is heavy and quite difficult to work. It has good water-holding capacity.

Sandy. Sandy soils are light and easy to work with. They are not water-retentive.

Loam soils. The ideal garden soil, which is a mixture of clay, sand and humus.

Acid or alkaline. In addition soils can be either acid, neutral or alkaline. An alkaline soil has a high lime or chalk content while an acid soil is low in lime. Thin sandy or chalky soils must have a liberal dressing of organic matter, a bucketful per square yard being a rough guide. This organic matter should be incorporated in the top spit of soil preferably by digging or using a mechanical cultivator. Double digging is never necessary for shrubs. Indeed, if the soil is reasonably well-drained, it is possible to plant directly into grassland or wasteland providing the weeds have first been removed with a modern herbicide. Waterlogged soils must be drained; try using drainage tiles connected to a sump or nearby ditch. If drainage is difficult because there is no easy outlet for the drainage water, then it is possible to create raised beds by moving topsoil from other parts of the garden or by importing top soil from a nearby building site.

Choosing and planting

When choosing plants from a nursery or garden centre, there are certain points to watch for. Make sure that a shrub has sturdy stems and good green leaves. Yellowish leaves could mean that the plant is starved or suffering a mineral deficiency. The plant should be firm at the base, denoting a good sound root system; plants that are loose at soil level are likely to be poorly rooted. If the shrub is deciduous and chosen in winter, look for sturdy well-branched stems and plump or well-formed buds.

Buying plants

Plants from nurseries can come in several ways:

1. Bare root. The plant arrives with no soil round its roots. Bare-rooted plants should be planted immediately and, if very dry, should be watered before planting. This method is usually chosen for transportation by post as it is the lightest.

2. Balled root. Here the plant has been dug up with the original soil still round the roots. It is then wrapped in hessian or burlap to hold the soil in place. The shrub can be planted with the wrapping still in position but it is best removed first.

Sometimes polythene or plastic sheeting is used instead of hessian. When planting, the polythene sheeting should be carefully removed without disturbing the soil.

3. Containers. If the plant arrives in a container, remove the container carefully, keeping the soil round the roots.

Rootball: When planting the shrub or climber, make a hole larger than the rootball of the shrub. Loosen the soil at the bottom of the hole and work in some peat or decayed manure. Add more of

these substances with the soil as the hole is filled in. When the hole has been partly filled in, shake the shrub gently up and down to work the soil in between the roots.

Container-grown specimens. After shaking, firm the ground with the feet. Top up the hole and firm again, adding more soil to make the ground level. On light soil a slight depression can be left to facilitate watering.

The distance left between shrubs when planting depends on their ultimate height and spread. As a rough guide a distance equal to half the ultimate height is adequate.

Container-grown nursery stock can be planted at any time of the year unless the ground is frozen or waterlogged. If the soil is dry, it must be given a good soaking the day before planting. Plants lifted from the open ground can be transplanted only during the dormant season which usually extends from late autumn to early spring. Once again, the soil should not be frozen, snow-covered or waterlogged. If spring droughts are a feature of your area, then autumn planting if preferable.

Aftercare

Having taken care of soil and situation and safely planted the trees the rest is minimal maintenance. For the first year or two, watering will have to be carried out during dry spells. It is also an advantage to mulch annually in spring, using the same sort of organic matter recommended for the initial planting. A layer 1in (25.4mm) deep over the root area is sufficient. If growth is poor, a general fertilizer—2 to 3 ounces (56 to 85gms) per square yard (meter)—should be added to the mulch. Weeding will be a chore for a couple of seasons, but as the shrubs grow together, light will be excluded from the soil and very few weeds will thrive. The best plan is to underplant the larger shrubs with smaller or prostrate growing kinds which are quick-growing and can cover the ground rapidly. This is known as ground-cover and if correctly done will practically eliminate weeding.

Pruning

There is much written about the pruning of shrubs. It is safe to say that nearly all will flower and prosper if never touched, and certainly after an initial trim when planting. Providing young plants bought from a nursery are well-grown, most can be left for three or four years. Subsequent pruning should be merely to shape up the plant, for the beauty of a shrub is its own shape. Allow

it to develop freely. If you find that it is necessary to take off enormous chunks of a shrub to stop if from swamping everything else, you have planted too closely, and it is time to thin out altogether.

If it is necessary to keep a shrub to a certain size, then the following rules can be applied. Shrubs that flower in the spring should be pruned when the last blossom has faded, cutting the flowered shoot back to 2 to 3in (5 to 7.6cm) above its junction with the parent stem. Summer-flowering shrubs should be pruned in spring before young growth is made, once again removing the previous season's flowered wood. Certain shrubs produce bigger and better flowers if hard-pruned each year, *Buddleia davidii*, *Spiraea japonica*, *S.X bumalda* and *Caryopteris X clandonesis* being popular examples. Begin hard pruning the first year of planting, cutting back to 6in (15cm) above ground level the first spring. In subsequent years, the stems should be cut back to about 4in (10cm) above their point of origin. However, this is often not really necessary — for example it is frequently stated that forsythia benefits from hard pruning after flowering, but it seldom receives this treatment and still smothers itself with blossom.

Climbers and wall shrubs require more attention to keep them neat and tidy. Once the climbing plant has covered its alloted space, surplus growth should be removed to its point of origin. Spring and summer-flowering species can be treated in the same way as free-standing shrubs. Plants such as *Clematis montana* and *Wisteria sinensis* which send out long climbing shoots each summer should have these pinched back to about 4in (10cm) once they get 12 to 18in (30 to 46cm) long. This can be done at intervals throughout the summer and helps to promote the formation of flowering buds for the next year.

The large-flowered hybrid clematis such as 'Nelly Moser', 'Hagley Hybrid' and 'Etoile Violette' can present difficulties to the novice pruner. Although they can grow over a tree stump or through a living tree without attention, when grown on walls they need regular pruning to prevent the formation of tangled masses. They normally flower in late summer and may be cut back early each spring to within a few inches of the parent stem. Hybrids of the species *florida*, *lanuginosa* and *patens*, which flower in late spring, should be pruned after the last flower has fallen, removing only the flowered growths and stems that are not required.

Sometimes a young shrub has not been prepared or initially trained in the nursery. Often it will branch and produce a good bush without special training. If it does not, then the strongest stems should be cut back by half or two-thirds every winter or spring until the desired number of branches has formed.

Overgrown and neglected shrubs should have all the old twiggy stems removed down to the base so that light and air can penetrate them. If necessary, the remaining branches can be shortened, particularly those stems that have flowered.

The temperate zone

The term *temperate zone* is used throughout this book to cover all parts of the world outside the tropical, sub-tropical and polar regions. Within it can be found a great range of climates which are distinguished by the fact that there are always marked differences between the seasons. Everywhere within the zone the average of the warmest month rises to at least 50°F (10°C) and there is always a possibility of temperatures falling to below freezing 32°F (0°C) at some time during the winter. As a general rule, the further away from the influence of the sea, the greater the extremes of temperature (which can range from -50°F (-45°C) to + 120°F (+48°C) in Central Asia and North America) while the rainfall decreases in reliability. Mountain ranges emphasize these differences strongly.

The critical factor with most shrubs is the amount of cold they can endure. The entries on the 150 shrubs illustrated indicate the minimum temperatures each variety can withstand; for other shrubs check with your local nursery. This is a good reason why it is more satisfactory to buy from a local nursery rather than to order by mail from another area: if a shrub prospers in the climate of your local nursery, so will it in your garden.

Aspect

Few garden owners are able to select the aspect of their garden, but if a choice is possible, it should be a gentle slope facing the sun. If you live in an area with persistent hot dry breezes or cold searing winds, shelter is a great advantage. If a hedge, fence, wall or row of trees does not offer protection already, then it is advisable to plant some sort of windbreak. The alternative is to use only shrubs that tolerate windy sites at first and, as they mature, interplant with less tolerant sorts. The sheltered side of a house can also be used for shrubs that require protection.

Winter protection

It is best to avoid growing shrubs proven to be tender in your home area. There are invariably alternative species just as lovely that will be hardy. If tender shrubs must be grown outdoors, however, there are several measures to take to protect them. First, a sheltered site away from strong cold winds must be found. Freezing winds in particular are lethal to tender plants. A site with a sunny aspect is best, preferably against a wall or fence over 6ft (1.8m) tall. In late autumn, or before cold weather is expected, lag the stems with wheat straw or bracken, using hessian (burlap) or sacking and string to hold it in place. In really cold sites mound weathered ashes, coarse sand or peat around the base to insure that if the top growth is killed, young shoots will arise from ground level.

Shrubs in the open ground may be protected in the following way. Spread strips of chicken wire as wide as the shrub is tall with a 4in (10cm) layer of bracken or straw and cover with another piece of chicken wire the same size. Secure this sandwich with wire or twine and stand it around the plant like a collar. A lid of similar construction can be placed on top during the coldest spells. In the less cold areas, heavy-duty polythene (plastic) sheeting can be used to cover tender plants, while bags are useful for free-standing specimens. If bags are used, holes must be made for ventilation or severe condensation will result, and stems or the whole plant may rot rather than be protected from cold.

Pests and diseases

Generally speaking, shrubs are remarkably free of pests and diseases. Among pests likely to be a nuisance — if only occasionally — are aphids or greenfly and caterpillars. Aphids suck the sap and often cause crippling of leaves and young stems. Caterpillars eat holes in leaves. Several brands of insecticides which include derris and malathion will deal with these pests. They should be used to manufacturer's instructions.

The only really serious shrub disease is known as honey fungus or bootlace fungus. The first symptoms are a sudden collapse of the leaves on a whole branch or the whole shrub. In the case of the latter, dig up and burn the shrub. If only one branch is effected, water its roots with Armillotox or other product manufactured for this purpose.

Bootlace fungus takes the form of tough, blackish, bootlace-like growths that spread underground from one tree or bush to the next, and if the whole bush dies, the soil must be treated before replanting.

Supporting climbers

Unlike shrubs and trees, which may need supporting only when they are young, climbers need support for life. This can be provided in various ways. The most natural method is to use a tree, living or dead. For example, an old apple tree can look very picturesque with a clematis rambling through it, and if the climber is not too vigorous no harm will come to the tree. Taller trees make fine hosts for self-clinging climbers like *Hydrangea petiolaris* or a tall-growing rose such as *Rosa filipes*.

Free-standing pillars, arbours or pergolas, fences and walls are the usual means of support for most climbers in the garden. Walls and fences will need trellis, wire or string attached for the plants to twine round, unless one choses self-clinging plants such as ivy, *Hydrangea petiolaris* or *Schizophragma hydrangeoides*. Small climbers will be happy growing over a wigwam of bean poles or pea sticks.

Containers

Shrubs grown permanently in pots, tubs or other containers require more attention than those in the open ground. Particular attention must be paid to watering. Do not depend on rainfall, even when the garden soil is thoroughly moist. The roots of a shrub in a container are concentrated into a small area and not spread out into surrounding soil. Also, the foliage of a container-grown plant often overlaps the rim and rain tends to be shed from leaves at the stem tips. During the growing season, an established potted plant will need watering several times a week. It is important to water thoroughly, enough so that a little surplus runs out of the bottom.

Feeding is also necessary for shrubs in containers. During the main growing season, from late spring to mid-summer, it is advisable to give weekly doses of a good brand-name liquid plant food at watering time.

In winter, if a shrub is known to be tender in your area, it is advisable to place it in a frost-free place. If the plant is deciduous, it can be stood in a shed or garage. If it is evergreen, it is best to place it in a greenhouse or sunny room. A night temperature of 35°F (2C°) is adequate and it should not be above 45°F (7°C) during the dormant winter period.

overall shape & habit

Shape and texture are important factors when planning a shrub garden. Narrow columnar or pyramidal forms are useful as accent points, drawing the eye to a particular area or planting scheme in the garden. Compact and rounded plants make their impact by providing contrast to more diffuse or slender habited shrubs. Arching and pendulous growth forms also provide contrast and are particularly effective combined with the pyramidal and columnar. Shrubs with a horizontal or totally prostrate and ground-hugging habit are mainly of use as ground cover between the taller kinds. Not only do they make a labour-saving weed smotherer, but they provide a pleasing background. They can also be used for clothing banks and open areas.

Strong, narrow upright lines
Shrubs
Berberis thunbergii 'Erecta'
Prunus 'Amanogawa'
P. X hillieri 'Spire'
P. 'Umineko'
Sorbus 'Joseph Rock'
S. aucuparia 'Fastigiata'
Ulmus sarniensis 'Aurea'
Malus 'Van Eseltine'
Conifers
Juniperus virginiana 'Skyrocket'
J. communis 'Hibernica'

Rounded compact growth
Shrubs
Acer palmatum 'Dissectum'
A. p. 'Dissectum Atropurpureum'
Ceanothus papillosus roweanus
Choisya ternata
Cistus in variety
Cotinus coggygria 'Royal Purple'
Cotoneaster conspicuus 'Highlight'
Cytisus praecox
Hebe albicans
H. 'Marjorie'
Lavandula 'Hidcote'
Philadelphus 'Manteau d'Hermine'
Potentilla 'Elizabeth'
P. fruticosa 'Tangerine'
Rhododendron 'Britannia'
Santolina chamaecyparissus
Senecio greyi

Hebe salicifolia (shrubby veronica)

Scrophulariaceae (foxglove family) New Zealand
This evergreen shrubby veronica is variable and readily forms hybrids with allied species. The plant portrayed is possibly of hybrid origin. *Hebe salicifolia* can grow to over 6ft (1.8m) in height. It has opposite pairs of pale green, slender-pointed willow-like leaves 4in (10cm) or more long. From mid-summer to early autumn white or palest purple flowers are borne in slender spikes. It will grow in any ordinary well-drained garden soil. Hardy in much of the temperate zone, it can be killed to ground level if severe cold periods are prolonged.

Chamaecyparis pisifera 'Plumosa Aurea Compacta'

Cupressaceae (cypress family) Japan
The Sawara cypress of Japan is an elegant tree up to 100ft (30m) or more which has given rise to many dwarf forms under 3ft (.9m) in height. Foliage varies from dark green to blue-green and can be variegated yellow or white. The Plumosa group have soft plumes of slender awl-shaped foliage. 'Plumosa Aurea Compacta' is a small conical bush that takes many years to exceed 1ft (30cm) in height. The leaves are soft yellow through the year, brightest in spring. It is hardy in the temperate zone and thrives in any good garden soil, preferably peat enriched.

Abelia X grandiflora

Caprifoliaceae (honeysuckle family) garden hybrid
Of bushy and rounded habit with arching stems, this semi-evergreen grows to 4ft (1.2m) or more. The glossy, broadly elliptic leaves make a pleasing foil for the pink and white flower clusters, like small foxgloves, which appear from mid-summer to autumn in abundance. They are fragrant, particularly on warm days. This abelia is only hardy in the parts of the temperate zone free from long periods of frost: 15° to 20°F (-9° to -7°C) will severely damage young growth. In cold areas plant on sheltered but sunny walls. A wide range of soil types is tolerated.

Potentilla (syn. arbuscula.) 'Elizabeth' (shrubby cinquefoil)

Rosaceae (rose family) Europe, Asia and America
This is a very variable deciduous species, ranging in height from 1 to 6ft (.3 to 1.8m) with white, yellow or red-flushed flowers. Also known as *P.f. arbuscula*, 'Elizabeth' is now considered to be a hybrid. It forms a rounded bush up to 3ft (.9m) high and wide with small, fingered leaves and a long succession (from late spring to autumn) of bright yellow blossoms like small single roses. Hardy throughout the temperate zone, it will grow in any soil from chalk to peat or sand. It flowers best in a sunny site.

Acer palmatum 'Dissectum' (cut-leaved Japanese maple)

Aceraceae (maple family) Japan, China and Korea
Japanese maples are deciduous and renowned for their autumn colours and diversity of form. 'Dissectum' forms an umbrella shape up to 8ft (2.4m) or more but is slow-growing and long remains at half this. Each leaf is divided into 5 to 7 narrow, long-toothed, pale-green leaflets. More common is the purple-leaved *A. p.* 'Dissectum Atropurpureum'. Japanese maple thrives in neutral or acid soil and partial shade. It will grow in dry, chalky soils, but needs plenty of peat or leaf-mould added. It is hardy in the temperate zone.

Cytisus X praecox (Warminster broom)

Leguminosae (pea family) garden hybrid
Originating as a hybrid of white Spanish broom (*C. multiflorus*) and *C. purgans*, about 1867, this 5ft (1.5m) tall broom is a spectacular small shrub. It forms a green-twigged bush, which, like most true brooms, is leafless for most of the year. Tiny leaves appear in spring, but soon fall and the green stems take on their functions. In late spring each twig becomes wreathed with countless creamy pea-flowers. This broom is hardy in the temperate zone, though some damage may occur in areas of prolonged severe frosts. It grows in any good garden soil, including dry, limy and sandy ones.

Hebe salicifolia

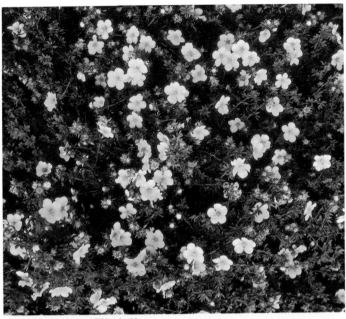

Potentilla fruticosa 'Elizabeth'

Chamaecyparis pisifera 'Plumosa Aurea Compacta'

Acer palmatum 'Dissectum'

Abelia X grandiflora

Cytisus X praecox

45

Conifers
Chamaecyparis lawsoniana 'Forsteckensis'
C. l. 'Gimbornii'
C. pisifera 'Filifera Aurea'
C. p. 'Boulevard' ('Cyanoviridis')
Cryptomeria japonica 'Elegans Nana'

Arching and pendulous branches
Shrubs
Berberis X stenophylla
Betula pendula 'Youngii'
Cytisus scoparius in variety
C. monspessulanus
Buddleia alternifolia
Genista cinerea
G. aetnensis
G. lydia
Potentilla fruticosa 'Primrose Beauty'
Rose species, particularly Rosa hugonis (or
    'Canary Bird'), californica 'Flore Plena',
    willmottiae
Salix purpurea 'Pendula'
S. caprea 'Pendula'
Spiraea X vanhouttei
Conifers
Juniperus X media 'Globosa Cinerea'
J. X m. 'Hetzii'
Podocarpus salignus
Taxus baccata 'Dovastonii Aurea'
T. b. 'Semperaurea'
Tsuga canadensis 'Bennett'

Horizontal growth or prostrate
    habit
Shrubs
Cotoneaster conspicuus 'Decorus'
C. horizontalis 'Variegatus'
C. 'Skogholm'
C. microphyllus cochleatus
C. X beanii
Cytisus scoparius 'Prostratus' (maritimus)
Potentilla fruticosa 'Longacre Variety'
Rosa 'Max Graff'
R. 'Raubritter'
R. X paulii
Conifers
Juniperus sabina 'Tamariscifolia'
J. X media 'Pfitzerana Glauca'
J. X m. 'Pfitzerana Aurea'
J. horizontalis 'Bar Harbor'
J. communis 'Depressa Aurea'
J. c. 'Effusa'
Picea abies 'Pseudoprostrata'
Tsuga canadensis 'Prostrata'

Genista lydia (Lydian broom)

Leguminosae (pea family) E. Balkans
This bright, attractive evergreen broom forms 2ft (61cm) tall hummocks of slender arching branches, the tips of which often touch the soil. Young stems are green with small leaves. In late spring and early summer, every stem becomes wreathed in clusters of bright yellow pea-shaped flowers so that not a twig can be seen. Any well-drained soil is suitable. The site must be a sunny one for a good show of blossoms. *Genista lydia* is not fully hardy in the temperate zone, temperatures below 5°F (-15°C) causing damage and sometimes death. In the colder areas it is best planted at the foot of a sheltered wall.

Spiraea X vanhouttei

Rosaceae (rose family) garden hybrid
Fully hardy in the temperate zone, this decorative hybrid deciduous shrub arose from the crossing of *Spiraea cantoniensis* from China and *S. trilobata* from N. Asia. It forms a vigorous bush of 5ft (1.5m) or more in height with a dense mass of slender arching stems. Young leaves are bright green and cleft into shallow lobes. In early summer, dense rounded clusters of tiny, glistening white flowers wreath every stem. Any well-drained soil is suitable. A sunny site is best, but partial shade is acceptable. This shrub is also suitable for containers and forces well in a cool greenhouse in spring.

Kolkwitzia amabilis (beauty bush)

Caprifoliaceae (honeysuckle family) China
Eventually reaching 7 or 8ft (2 to 2.4m) high and wide, this vigorous deciduous shrub has spreading and arching branchlets with leaves of a pleasing matt green. In late spring the tubular blossoms are borne in abundance. Each blossom is an exquisite shade of pale, almost luminous pink, highlighted by a yellow throat. For most prolific blooming, a sunny site is best, but partial shade is tolerated. Any fertile soil is suitable. There is a superb, darker pink form known as 'Pink Cloud'. It is hardy in the temperate zone.

Berberis darwinii (Darwin's barberry)

Berberidaceae (barberry family) Chile, Argentina
This is one of the finest of the evergreen barberries, with arching and elegant growth. It was first seen by Darwin in 1835 during his voyage in H.M.S. Beagle. Well-grown plants can attain a height of 10ft (3m), but 6 to 8ft (1.8 to 2.4m) is a good average. In spring, all the shoots are wreathed in clusters of small, cup-shaped, bright orange blossoms. Any fertile soil suites this South American barberry, and it is reasonably hardy in the temperate zone. However, temperatures below 0°F (-18°C) may damage or kill the shoots. It does well in partial shade or full sun.

Buddleia alternifolia

Loganiaceae (buddleia family) China
Naturally a large shrub up to 10ft (3m) or so, this deciduous *Buddleia* is usually grown in gardens as a small tree with a single trunk. In this form its naturally weeping habit with slender arching stems can be seen to full advantage. An ideal specimen tree for the smaller lawn, it is particularly effective in early summer when wreathed in small, compact clusters of fragrant lilac-purple blossoms. *Buddleia alternifolia* can also be grown as an unusual cover for a large wall. It is hardy in the temperate zone and will grow in any ordinary well-drained garden soil.

Cotoneaster conspicuus

Rosaceae (rose family) S.E. Tibet
There are several cultivated forms of this evergreen shrub, the best for covering banks and other difficult features being 'Decorus', illustrated here. It forms arching stems spreading to several feet in length but rarely exceeds 4ft (1.2m) in height. In early summer each two-year-old stem becomes massed with tiny bowl-shaped white flowers. These are followed by red pea-sized berries which ripen in early autumn. Any good garden soil is suitable, but a sunny site is necessary for a good fruit crop. It is hardy in the temperate zone, though in very cold winters it may lose all its leaves.

Genista lydia

Berberis darwinii

Spiraea X vanhouttei

Buddleia alternifolia

Kolkwitzia amabilis

Cotoneaster conspicuus

47

fragrant flowers & foliage

Unless one is completely 'scent-blind', fragrance is always appreciated in the garden. Shrubs can provide pleasing aromas from both flower and leaf. Scents, like colours, are very personal; the fragrance enjoyed by one person may be the abomination of another. By choosing the right species, it is easy to please varying tastes, ranging from sweet perfumes, piney tangs to the savory smells of sage and curry plant. Moreover, these scents can be had the year round. In winter there are the spicily sweet aromas of winter-sweet (*Chimonanthus praecox*) and Chinese witch hazel (*Hamamelis mollis*). Spring brings us several very fragrant daphnes and the lilacs, while summer bears upon its warm airs the heady scents of honeysuckle, philadelphus and several shrub roses. Autumn has buddleia and throughout the year we have the fragrant foliages of lavender, rosemary, myrtle and sweet bay.

Fragrant flowers

Shrubs
Buddleia alternifolia
B. davidii
B. 'Lochinch'
Chimonanthus praecox
Cistus—most species
Daphne mezereum
D. X burkwoodii
D. collina neapolitana
Elaeagnus glabra
Hamamelis mollis
Lonicera syringantha 'Grandiflora'
Mahonia japonica
Philadelphus species and cultivars, particularly
    'Sybille', 'Virginal', 'Bouquet Blanc',
    delavayi
Pittosporum tobira
P. undulatum (mild area in U.K.)
Shrub roses, particularly Hybrid Musks 'Cornelia' 'Penelope', 'Buff Beauty' and :-
Bourbon and Old Fashioned Roses
Syringa persica
S. vulgaris in variety
Viburnun X burkwoodii
V. X bodnantense
V. farreri (fragrans)
V. X juddii

Choisya ternata (Mexican orange blossom)

Rutaceae (orange family) Mexico
An evergreen shrub, usually compact and rounded, which can grow to 6ft (1.8m) in height and girth, it is easily maintained at 4 to 5ft (1.2 to 1.5m) by pruning after flowering. Clusters of orange-blossom-scented flowers appear during spring with intermittant sprays until late autumn. Although hardy in most of the temperate zone, freezing winds will scorch the foliage and can kill shoots. Prolonged periods of temperatures below 20°F (-7°C) can kill. A wide range of soils are tolerated, but thin chalky ones should be enriched with manure, peat, compost or leaf-mould.

Buddleia davidii 'Royal Red' (butterfly bush)

Loganiaceae (buddleia family) China
If allowed to grow unrestrained, this shrub can attain a height and spread of 8 to 10ft (2.4 to 3m). But with hard annual pruning in spring, it forms an erect shrub of 6ft (1.8m) or so with strong arching-tipped stems. The deciduous leaves are grey-green and similar to a large willow. From late summer into autumn, dense, slender trusses of tubular blossoms are borne. Several garden varieties are available in a range of shades from white and lavender to blue and red-purples. It is hardy in the temperate zone and will thrive in almost any well-drained soil.

Syringa X hyacinthiflora 'Buffon'

Oleaceae (olive family) garden hybrid
Sometimes classified under the common lilac heading (*S. vulgaris*), this early flowering, deciduous hybrid can reach 10ft (3m), but takes several years to do so. It also responds to moderate pruning after flowering. The leaves are heart-shaped and clusters of four-petalled, soft pink flowers appear in spring — a little earlier than common Lilac. It will grow in any fertile garden soil and is hardy in the temperate zone. There are several other forms of this hybrid lilac: 'Alice Eastwood' has rosy purple flowers; 'Blue Hyacinth' is mauve to blue; while 'Purple Heart' has large, purple florets.

Rosa X 'Fritz Nobis'

Rosaceae (rose family) garden hybrid
The parents of this modern shrub rose are the large-flowered form of the eglantine (*R. rubiginosa* 'Magnifica') and 'Joanna Hill', a pre-war pink hybrid now no longer grown. 'Fritz Nobis' is of medium vigour, reaching about 5ft (1.5m) in height. The rich green foliage is a pleasing foil for the double salmon-pink flowers with their light sweet fragrance. Persistent dark red hips follow the flowers, which do not reappear after the midsummer flush. 'Fritz Nobis' grows well on its own roots and does not need to be grafted. It thrives in any fertile soil and is hardy in the temperate zone.

Osmanthus delavayi

Oleaceae (olive family) N. China
This evergreen is a must for gardeners who love fragrance and white flowers. Growing slowly to 6ft (1.8m) tall with a similar spread, it has an arching mode of growth which sets off the profusion of small, waxy-white, tubular blossoms perfectly. Clusters of buds appear in winter and open in spring. Any fertile, reasonably well-drained soil is suitable, providing it does not dry out excessively. A sunny or partially shaded site is equally good. It is hardy in the temperate region. Since introduced from China in 1890, this shrub has had all major awards from the Royal Horticultural Society.

Corylopsis willmottiae

Hamamelidaceae (witch hazel family) W. China
Of rounded outline, bushy and slender-twigged, this attractive deciduous shrub can reach 6ft (1.8m) in height. It is, however, relatively slow-growing and takes some years to reach this size. In early spring, pendant spikes of cup-shaped, soft-yellow flowers appear and scent the air around. Best growth is made on moisture-retentive but well-drained soil that is acid or neutral. Alkaline soils are suitable only if well enriched with peat or leaf-mould. It is hardy in the temperate zone and will thrive in sun or partial shade.

Salvia officinalis 'Tricolor' (coloured or variegated sage)

Labiatae (mint family) S. Europe
The common green-leaved sage is a popular herb among cooks. However, its compact rounded shape and aromatic evergreen foliage with a pleasing grey matt finish make it a worthy ornament. This is even more true of its variegated forms 'Icterina' and 'Tricolor'. The latter develops stems 1ft (30cm) tall in summer which bear tubular, hooded blue-purple flowers. If the flowering spikes and a short piece of the supporting stems are removed every autumn the bushes remain under 2ft (61cm). Any well-drained garden soil is suitable and it will thrive in the temperate zone.

Rosmarinus officinalis (rosemary)

Labiatae (mint and dead-nettle family) S. Europe and Asia Minor
A culinary herb for many centuries, rosemary is a fragrant, decorative evergreen shrub. Of several distinctive variants, the commonest in gardens is an erect, bushy form 4ft (1.2m) or more. The very narrow leaves are densely borne and in the axils bear tubular flowers in spring and again in the autumn. Both leaves and flowers give off a sweet aroma when lightly bruised. Rosemary needs a sunny site and well-drained soil, acid or alkaline. It is hardy in much of the temperate zone, but may suffer damage if the temperature drops to 0°F (-18°C) and below.

Lippia citriodora (lemon scented verbena)

Verbenaceae (verbena family) Chile
Sometimes listed as *Aloysia citriodora*, this tender shrub can reach 6ft (1.8m) or more if grown against a wall. The willow shaped evergreen leaves have a strong sweet lemon aroma when lightly bruised. Tiny flowers are borne during late summer and early autumn. Any well-drained soil is suitable. The site must be sheltered and sunny, preferably against a wall, fence or evergreen hedge. Temperatures of 20°F (-7°C) will damage young stems and the plant may be killed to ground level at 15°F (-9°C). It makes a good container shrub in a frost-free place in winter.

Chamaecyparis lawsoniana 'Aureo-variegata'

Cupressaceae (cypress family) W. USA
Although capable of reaching 20ft (6m), this evergreen variegated form of Lawson cypress is compact in growth and easily kept in check by pinching out the leading shoot once or twice a year. The tiny scale-like leaves are pressed close to the twigs which in turn are arranged in flattened sprays. Each spray bears blotches of creamy yellow, which brighten up the normal, somewhat grey-green hue. Small globular cones are borne in late summer. This cypress will grow in any fertile soil providing it does not dry out. It is hardy in the temperate zone.

Cistus X purpureus (sun rose)

Cistaceae (rock and sun rose family) garden hybrid
All the many different kinds of sun rose are decorative garden plants, but are not reliably hardy in the temperate zone. Freezing winds and temperatures that fall to 15°F (-9°C) for lengthy periods will damage or kill plants unless protected with straw or bracken matting. *Cistus X purpureus* forms a round evergreen bush up to 4ft (1.2m) or so, with hoary, narrow green leaves that have a pleasing matt finish. Flowers, about 3in (7.6cm) across, appear around mid-summer. A sunny site and well-drained soil are essential for success. It stands drought and sea winds well.

Lavandula spica 'Hidcote' (lavender)

Labiatae (mint family) Mediterranean
Among the many sorts of lavender, 'Hidcote' ranks high. It makes a compact bush, seldom more than 1ft (30cm) tall, clad with narrow, bright grey-green evergreen leaves that give off the lavender fragrance when bruised and at all times if kept warm and dry. During the summer, 1ft (30cm) tall flowering stems appear, bearing spikes of tubular violet-purple blossoms. This lavender is hardy in the temperate zone, though it may suffer in prolonged severe winters. It will grow in any well-drained soil. To keep the bushes compact and healthy, it is best to cut back the flowering stems each autumn.

Aromatic foliage
Shrubs
Cistus pulverulentus
C. 'Silver Pink'
C. villosus
C. parviflorus
C. ladanifer
Eucalyptus (grown as shrubs)
Helichrysum serotinum
Illicium anisatum
Laurus nobilis (bay laurel or sweet bay)
Lavandula spica in variety
Lippia citriodora (lemon-scented verbena)
Myrica gale (acid soil)
Myrtus communis and cultivars
Rhododendron—small-leaved species and particularly:-
R. impeditum
R. calostrotum
R. augustinii
R. saluenense
R. 'Blue Tit'
R. 'Blue Diamond'
Rosmarinus officinalis in variety particularly:-
R. o. 'Fastigatus'
R. o. 'Severn Sea'
Ruta graveolens 'Jackman's Blue'
Salvia grahamii
S. officinalis 'Tricolor'
S. o. 'Icterina'
Conifers
Most have aromatic foliage when crushed, particularly dwarf and medium-growing species and cultivars of:-
Chamaecyparis
Cupressus
Juniperus
Picea sitchensis
Thuja plicata

Choisya ternata

Rosa X 'Fritz Nobis'

Buddleia davidii 'Royal Red'

Osmanthus delavayi

Syringa X hyacinthiflora 'Buffon'

Corylopsis willmottiae

50

Salvia officinalis 'Tricolor'

Chamaecyparis lawsoniana

Rosmarinus officinalis

Cistus X purpureus

Lippia citriodora

Lavandula spica 'Hidcote'

51

dry sunny sites

Although much of the temperate zone has its rainfall scattered throughout the year, there are always dry areas which present a problem. The following plants can be grown in dry areas without continuous watering. Quite often, these dry areas may be very small such as a border against the leeside of a free-standing or house wall. Such a border, being effectually in a rain shadow, can be astonishingly dry, while the soil a foot or two away is quite moist and capable of growing a wide range of plants. Several types of plants will grow in such dry sites, among them a considerable number of decorative shrubs. When first planted in position the young shrubs will need to be kept moist until well-established. If planted in early autumn it should be sufficient to give a good soaking once or twice before winter. Spring-planted specimens will need constant attention throughout the coming summer, especially if it is drier than usual.

Shrubs

Buddleia fallowiana
Ceanothus 'Gloire de Versailles'
C. thyrsiflorus 'Repens'
Cistus species in variety
Genista lydia
Halimium ocymoides
H. lasianthum
Helianthemum in variety
Indigofera gerardiana
Kerria japonica 'Variegata'
Lavandula stoechas
Phlomis fruticosa
Potentilla fruticosa
Rosa nitida
R. pimpinellifolia
Yucca gloriosa
Y. recurvifolia
and most grey-leaved shrubs

Convolvulus cneorum

Convolvulaceae (morning glory family) E. Europe

Barely exceeding 1½ft (46cm) tall, this low-growing decorative evergreen forms wide hummocks 2ft (61cm) or more when happily situated. The narrow leaves are bright silver-grey, with a sheen when young. In late spring terminal clusters of wide, funnel-shaped white flowers are borne and, after the main flush, appear off and on until autumn. It will grow in any sharply-drained soil, but the site must be sunny or the plant will straggle and flower poorly. It is not hardy in the colder parts of the temperate zone and will be severely damaged or killed if the temperature drops to 0°F (-18°C).

Cytisus battandieri (Moroccan broom)

Leguminosae (pea family) Morocco

This evergreen broom has leaves covered with silky white hairs that impart a grey sheen to the bush. Deep-yellow pea-shaped flowers that smell of pineapples are borne in summer. A well-grown bush can attain 6 to 8ft (1.8 to 2.4m) high and wide, with long arching branches. It lends itself to training on walls, and in colder areas this is the best way to grow it. Any well-drained soil is suitable and the site must be sunny. Although hardy in most of the temperate regions, freezing winds will defoliate stems and shoots will be killed. Temperatures below 0°F (-18°C) can kill it to ground level.

Spartium junceum (Spanish broom)

Leguminosae (pea family) Mediterranean

Spartium is largely leafless with bright green stems. True leaves are borne but soon fall. Vigorous and erect, it can quickly attain 6ft (1.8m) in height, and by means of annual pruning this height can be kept for several years. During the summer and autumn a succession of bright yellow honey-scented pea-flowers are borne in erect spikes. *Spartium* grows in any well-drained soil, but needs a sunny site for maximum flowering. It is not reliably hardy throughout the temperate zone, as it is damaged or killed by freezing winds and temperatures below 0°F (-18°C).

Helianthemum nummularium (rock rose)

Cistaceae (rock and sun rose family) Europe

The evergreen rock rose thrives in poor soil and is an invaluable ground cover in conditions too dry for other plants. Most forms are of low-growing or prostrate growth habit. The flowers range from yellow and orange to crimson and white and there are double-flowered kinds. The first flowers occur in early summer, with sporadic blooming into autumn. Secondary blooming can be increased by cutting back flower stems as soon as all petals have fallen. Rock roses are only hardy in the milder parts of the temperate zone; below 0°F (-18°C) they can be killed.

Yucca recurvifolia

Liliaceae (lily family) E. USA

Hardly shrubs in the accepted sense, the yuccas are characterized by a stout trunk with a few branches, each topped by a dense rosette of sword-shaped evergreen leaves. They have a palm-like quality which lends an exotic touch to the temperate scene. This description is typical of *Y. recurvifolia* (though some species of *Yucca* do not produce trunks). Well-grown plants can be 6ft (1.8m) tall, but are slow-growing. In late summer, dense, narrowly pyramidal clusters of pendant creamy-white bells, up to 6ft (1.8m) tall, are produced. Yucca grows in any well-drained garden soil and is hardy in the temperate zone.

Ceratostigma willmottianum (hardy plumbago)

Plumbaginaceae (plumbago family) W. China

Despite the name, this deciduous shrub is not completely hardy throughout the temperate zone. Temperatures of 10°F (-12°C) will usually kill top growth, but shoots quickly grow from the base in spring. Indeed, the stems of a low bush of 2ft (61cm) or so may be cut to ground level each spring. In late summer into autumn, rich blue flower clusters appear, ceasing with the first severe frost. The leaves often take on red tints before they die. A well-drained fertile soil is needed and a sheltered site in full sun gives the best floral display.

Convolvulus cneorum

Helianthemum nummularium

Cytisus battandieri

Yucca recurvifolia

Spartium junceum

Ceratostigma willmottianum

53

shady sites

Shady sites in a garden seem to present a problem to many gardeners when it comes to finding suitable plants to grow. Shrubs can easily solve this problem, for there are many that are shade-tolerant or which thrive best in diffused light. Some of the most attractive shrubs come within this category, including camellia and rhododendron. The most difficult sites are those immediately under large, shallow-rooted trees or against high shaded walls. Both aspects have the added disadvantage of dry soil conditions, at least for part of the year. Extra watering will be essential for a season after planting and the site under trees will need mulching with compost or manure.

Shrubs

Aucuba japonica
Buxus sempervirens
Camellia japonica in variety
Danae racemosa
Euonymus japonicus and cultivars
E. fortunei and cultivars
Fatshedera lizei
Fatsia japonica
Hypericum calycinum
Ilex aquifolium in variety
Mahonia aquifolium 'Atropurpurea'
Prunus laurocerasus 'Otto Luyken'
Rhododendron in great variety (acid soil)
Ruscus aculeatus
Skimmia japonica
Symphoricarps — all species
Viburnum davidii

X Gaulnettya wisleyensis

Ericaceae (heather family) garden origin
The parents of this interesting bi-generic hybrid are the western North American *Gaultheria shallon* and the southern South American *Pernettya mucronata*. It forms a dense bushy thicket of suckering stems up to 2ft (61cm) tall clad with narrow, leathery evergreen leaves. In late spring and early summer clusters of small white bell-flowers are profusely borne at the ends of the shoots, followed by dark red berries that persist all winter. Moisture-retentive soil which is lime-free is essential, and it is hardy in all but the coldest parts of the temperate zone.

Hedera helix 'Congesta' (dwarf bush ivy)

Araliaceae (ivy family) garden variety
Most ivies creep over the ground or climb trees or walls. Even the so-called bush ivies have a climbing juvenile stage. 'Congesta' stands apart, having no climbing shoots. It forms an erect evergreen bush up to 1½ft (46cm) tall and sometimes as much as 3ft (91cm) and has a distinctive shape and texture, with small triangular to heart-shaped dark green lustrous leaves crowded along the stems. It will grow in any well-drained soil and tolerates shade well, though partial shade is best for compact growth. It is hardy in the temperate zone, but severe wind frosts or temperatures below 0°F (-18°C) may damage it.

Mahonia aquifolium (Oregon grape)

Berberidaceae (barberry family) W. USA
This erect evergreen suckering shrub can grow to 6ft (1.8m) in height but usually stops at half that. Each stem has few branches and forms clumps of glossy dark-green foliage. The leaves are composed of 7 or more spiny leaflets which take on bronze or coppery hues in winter. In early spring, terminal clusters of bright yellow cup-shaped flowers appear, followed by edible black-purple berries. It thrives in any fertile soil and tolerates deep shade, though some sun is needed for good blooming. It is hardy in the temperate zone, though freezing winds may scorch leaves and kill young shoots.

Hypericum elatum 'Elstead'

Guttiferae (St. John's wort family) garden origin
It is now known that the garden shrub of this name is a hybrid of tutsan (*H. androsaemum*) and *H. hircinum* and should be known as *H.X inodorum*. Capable of attaining 5ft (1.5m) in height, but usually much less, this deciduous shrub is erect and well-branched with smoothly oval to slightly oblong, bright green leaves. Small pale yellow flowers with a prominent boss of stamens are borne in terminal clusters during the summer, followed by berry-like fruits which turn brilliant salmon-red in autumn. Any fertile well-drained soil is suitable. It is hardy in the temperate zone.

Paeonia suffruticosa (moutan or tree peony)

Paeoniaceae (peony family) China
Among the many cultivars of the deciduous tree peony are both single and double-flowered sorts in a wide range of shades. The double forms resemble large full-blown roses and are the ones most favoured in gardens. The single-flowered, with their large bowl-shaped blossoms, are not so long-lasting. Sparingly and robustly branched, tree peonies can attain 6ft (1.8m) in height. They are hardy in the temperate zone though the young shoots are scorched by spring frost if not grown beneath trees. Any fertile soil is suitable, preferably enriched with leaf-mould.

Cornus controversa 'Variegata' (wedding cake tree)

Cornaceae (dogwood family) China, Japan
Although slow-growing, this highly ornamental deciduous species eventually makes a slim tree up to 10ft (3m) or more. The slender erect trunk carries distinct layers of small branches with silvery-white variegated leaves. Small creamy white flowers appear in late spring. A neutral or acid moisture-retentive soil is best, but alkaline ones are suitable if enriched with leaf-mould or peat. It is hardy in the temperate zone. Although it will grow in sun or shade, a partially shaded site seems to give the best results.

X Gaulnettya wisleyensis

Hypericum elatum 'Elstead'

Hedera helix 'Congesta'

Paeonia suffruticosa

Mahonia aquifolium

Cornus controversa 'Variegata'

55

container shrubs

Nowadays, patios and terraces are gaining in popularity among the owners of smaller gardens. They make pleasant places to sit out in, even after heavy rain when grass would still be too wet. Paved areas of this kind need the softening effect of plants, and containers of varied design are now available specifically for this purpose. Although a wide range of plants can be grown in containers, shrubs rank among the ideal candidates, being long-lived and requiring little attention other than regular watering and feeding. Adequate watering is very important. All too often one sees a container-grown shrub wilting even after a shower of rain. It must be recognized that when the root system of a plant is concentrated into a container it needs considerably more water per square surface area.

Shrubs

Acacia baileyana
Acer palmatum (partial shade)
Albizia julibrissin 'Rosea'
Aralia elata 'Variegata'
Camellia japonica in variety
Caragana arborescens 'Lorbergii'
Choisya ternata
Eucalyptus gunnii and others
Fatsia japonica
Garrya elliptica
G. laurifolia macrophylla
Hebe 'Alicia Amherst'
H. X franciscana 'Blue Gem'
H. 'Purple Queen'
Hydrangea macrophylla Hortensia in variety
H. Lacecap in variety
H. X paniculata 'Grandiflora'
Lagerstroemia indica 'Rosea'
Metrosideros diffusa and others
Nerium oleander
Pittosporum colensoi
P. tenuifolium
Pseudopanax arboreus
P. laetus
Rhododendrons in variety (partial shade)

Climbers

Hedera (ivies) in variety
Jasminum officinale
J. polyanthum
Lonicera japonica 'Aureoreticulata'
L. periclymenum 'Serotina'
L. sempervirens 'Superba'

Hydrangea macrophylla 'Blue Wave' (blue lacecap)

Hydrangeaceae (hydrangea family) Japan
All the comments regarding *Hydrangea macrophylla* Hortensia also apply to the Lacecap group. But these have a flattened head of florets composed of numerous tiny fertile florets surrounded by a ring of sterile ones. In the case of 'Blue Wave', the central florets are a steely blue and the sterile ones are gentian blue when grown in an acid soil. However, in soils ranging from neutral to alkaline the florets appear in shades of purple through to pink. It does well in light woodland and by the sea and has the same hardiness rating as the *Hortensias*.

Chamaecyparis obtusa 'Aurea' (golden Hinoki cypress)

Cupressaceae (cypress family) Japan
Hinoki cypress is an important timber tree in Japan and held sacred by followers of the Shinto faith. It is broadly conical in outline with flattened sprays of tiny evergreen scale-like leaves. *Chamaecyparis obtusa* 'Aurea' is more slow-growing and in containers can easily be kept to a few feet in height. The leaves are golden yellow and are a particularly rich shade in winter. It is hardy in the temperate zone and tolerates a wide range of soils. In containers it is important to see that that the plant never dries out, or browning of the foliage will occur.

Fuchsia 'Traudchen Bonstedt'

Onagraceae (evening primrose and fuchsia family) garden hybrid
Herr Bonstedt hybridized the wild Caribbean *Fuchsia F. triphylla* with other species and produced garden varieties in shades of pink, red and orange. 'Traudchen Bonstedt' has salmon pink blossoms and pale green foliage. It can attain 4ft (1.2m) or more in height. Except in the warmest parts of the temperate zone, it is not hardy outside in winter unless protected by glass, matting or a mound of weathered ashes or sand. Even then top growth will be cut down by frost, but it comes back from the base each spring. Any fertile soil is suitable.

Hydrangea macrophylla Hortensia (common hydrangea)

Hydrangeaceae (hydrangea family) Japan
The common mop-headed hydrangeas are deciduous, rarely exceeding 5ft (1.5m) and easily kept to 3 or 4ft (.9 to 1.2m) by annual pruning. From summer to autumn dense heads of broad sterile florets are borne in shades of white, pink, purple and blue. They tolerate a wide range of soils, but need acid soils for good blue flowers and alkaline for pink. A special blueing compound is available for containers. *Hydrangea macrophylla* grows well by the sea but needs protecting in the coldest parts of the temperate zone with matting or a mound of sand or peat.

Camellia X williamsii (Williams' camellia)

Theaceae (camellia and tea tree family)
In 1925, the noted gardener J. C. Williams crossed *Camellia japonica* with the Chinese *C. saluenensis*, a graceful species with dogrose-like flowers. The result was a range of charming vigorous evergreens up to 10ft (3m) tall with single or semi-double flowers ranging from white through shades of blush-pink to light red. They begin to flower in autumn and continue through winter into spring. Hardy in the temperate zone, a sheltered site or wall is advisable as the blossoms are damaged by less than 27°F (-3°C). An acid or neutral soil rich in humus is ideal.

Laurus nobilis (sweet bay or bay laurel)

Lauraceae (laurel family) Mediterranean
The sweet bay has been cultivated for several hundred years as a culinary and container shrub. The evergreen leaves have a sweet aromatic smell when bruised. The inconspicuous, fluffy flower clusters appear in spring and are followed by purple-black, ovoid, cherry-sized fruits. Left to grow naturally in sheltered sites, sweet bay can attain 10ft (3m) in height. However, it stands clipping well, and so can be kept at the height desired. Any well-drained soil is suitable and a site in sun or partial shade. Temperatures below 10°F (-12°C) can cause damage to leaves and young stems.

Hydrangea macrophylla 'Blue Wave'

Hydrangea macrophylla Hortensia

Chamaecyparis obtusa 'Aurea'

Camellia X williamsii

Fuchsia 'Traudchen Bonstedt'

Laurus nobilis

coloured foliage effects

Many plants, including some shrubs, are grown exclusively for their massed display of blossom or for the appeal of individually lovely flowers. Many of these plants have nothing else to offer once the flowering season has passed. Other plants are grown for the beauty of their foliage, and it is from these we must choose if long periods of interest are required. Shrubs, among all the plant categories, have the best foliage display. Some species have copper. purple or red leaves when young. *Pieris formosa forrestii*, for example, has young leaves of such a brilliant red that they are mistaken for flowers. The most useful shrubs however are those that have coloured leaves the whole growing season and, in the case of evergreens, the whole year. There are many of these in shades of yellow, red, purple, grey and silver, plus variegated combinations.

Grey or silver foliage
Shrubs
Artemisia arborescens
Atriplex halimus
Ballota pseudodictamnus
Calluna vulgaris 'Silver Queen'
Caryopteris X clandonensis
Cistus 'Silver Pink'
C. pulverulentus
Convolvulus cneorum
Cytisus battandieri
Dorycnium hirsutum
Elaeagnus angustifolia
Feijoa sellowiana
Halimium atriplicifolium
Hebe albicans
H. colensoi 'Glauca'
H. pinguifolia 'Pagei'
Lavandula spica
Leptospermum cunninghamii
L. lanigerum
Olearia X scilloniensis
Salix lanata
S. repens 'Argentea'
Senecio greyi
Teucrium fruticans
Potentilla fruticosa mandshurica
P. f. 'Vilmoriniana'
Santolina neapolitana
S. chamaecyparissus

Hebe pinguifolia 'Pagei'
Scrophulariaceae (speedwell and snapdragon family) New Zealand
Silvery blue-grey evergreen leaves distinguish this mat-forming shrublet. With a total height of 4in (10.2cm) and spread of 2 to 3ft (61 to 91cm) it is a good ground cover plant. Clusters of glistening white flowers are profuse in late spring and blooming shoots appear until autumn. Any good soil, either alkaline or acid, will suit this little *Hebe*. A sunny site is preferred, but it will grow well in partial shade. It is fairly hardy in the temperate region, but prolonged wind frosts will damage the shoots and temperatures below 10°F (-12°C) can be lethal.

Santolina chamaecyparissus (lavender cotton)
Compositae (daisy family) S. France, Pyrenees
Frequently used as an edging, this evergreen with its bright grey foliage blends well with bright-hued annual flowers. Although low, it gets straggly with age and is best cut to ground level each spring. It then produces compact 1ft (30cm) mounds with a spread of 1½ to 2ft (46 to 61cm). The bright yellow flower heads appear from late summer to autumn. A sunny site is necessary for best results, but any well-drained soil is suitable. While hardy in most temperate regions, prolonged periods of cold below 0°F (-18°C) can be fatal.

Elaeagnus X ebbingei
Elaeagnaceae (oleaster family) garden hybrid
This hybrid has oval-to-rounded evergreen leaves which are silvered beneath. The young leaves are also frosted above with silvery buff scales. Vigorous and robust, this shrub can attain 6ft (1.83m) in as many years and forms an excellent hedge or windbreak, especially near the sea. Clusters of honey-scented, silvery, bell-shaped flowers depend from the leaf axils in autumn. Any ordinary soil is suitable and both sunny and partially shaded sites. Although hardy in the temperate regions, prolonged wind frosts can damage leaves and young shoots.

Helianthemum nummularium 'Watergate Rose' (rock rose)
Cistaceae (rock and sun rose family)
Sometimes listed under the alternative specific names of *H. chamaecistus* and *H. vulgare*, 'Watergate Rose' is an evergreen of garden origin and likely to be a hybrid. It forms mats of oval leaves with a grey-green finish which make a pleasing background for the profusion of rose-crimson flowers. The main flush of blossoms is in mid-summer. Remove the summer flower stems as soon as the last bloom fades to encourage an autumn display. A sunny site and any well-drained soil spell success, but temperatures below 0°F (-18°C) can kill.

Rhododendron lepidostylum
Ericaceae (heather family) N. China
This neat dwarf rhododendron is well worth growing just for its foliage, which is composed of deciduous or semi-evergreen elliptic bristly leaves which are a bright blue-green. The shrub is of compact habit, seldom exceeding 2ft (61cm) in height. In late spring, pale yellow, funnel-shaped flowers are borne. Unlike many rhododendrons, this mountain dweller needs an open site to grow compactly and flower well. An acid soil that does not dry out is also a necessity. It is hardy in the temperate regions, but needs a cool position in the milder areas.

Senecio greyi
Compositae (daisy family) New Zealand
This shrub is sometimes confused with the allied *S. laxifolius*. Whatever the name, the evergreen will be compact and rounded, with leaves grey above and white-felted beneath. In summer, terminal clusters of bright yellow daisy flowers appear, with sporadic blooming into the autumn. Any well-drained soil is suitable and a site in full sun is needed for compact growth. This shrub is excellent for exposed places by the sea. Inland, it is not reliably hardy if the temperature drops below 0°F (-18°C). If killed to ground level, however, it usually sprouts from the base when warmer weather returns.

Hebe pinguifolia 'Pagei'

Helianthemum nummularium 'Watergate Rose'

Santolina chamaecyparissus

Rhododendron lepidostylum

Elaeagnus X ebbingei

Senecio greyi

59

(grey or silver foliage cont)

Conifers

Chamaecyparis lawsoniana 'Fletcheri'
C. l. 'Chilworth Silver'
C. l. 'Pembury Blue'
C. pisifera 'Boulevard'
Cupressus cashmeriana
C. glabra 'Pyramidalis'
Juniperus chinensis 'Obelisk'
J. 'Grey Owl'
J. X media 'Pfitzerana Glauca'
J. sabina 'Hicksii'
J. squamata 'Meyeri'
J. horizontalis 'Wiltonii' ('Blue Rug')

Golden and yellow foliage
Shrubs

Acer japonicum 'Aureum'
Berberis thunbergii 'Aurea'
Calluna vulgaris 'Aurea'
C. v. 'Joy Vanstone'
C. v. 'Serlei Aurea' and others
Hedera helix 'Buttercup' (climber)
Lonicera nitida 'Baggesen's Gold'
Philadelphus coronarius 'Aureus'
Physocarpus opulifolius 'Luteus'
Ribes sanguineum 'Brocklebankii'
Sambucus racemosa 'Plumosa Aurea'
Weigela X 'Looymansii Aurea'

Conifers

Chamaecyparis lawsoniana 'Lanei'
C. l. 'Lutea Nana'
C. l. 'Winston Churchill'
C. obtusa 'Crippsii'
C. o. 'Tetragona Aurea'
C. pisifera 'Filifera Aurea'
Juniperus X media 'Pfitzerana Aurea'
Taxus baccata 'Standishii'
Thuja occidentalis 'Rheingold'

Red or purple
Shrubs

Acer palmatum 'Dissectum Atropurpureum'
Berberis ottawensis 'Purpurea'
B. thunbergii 'Atropurpurea'
B. t. 'Atropurpurea Nana'
Brachyglottis repanda 'Purpurea'
Corylus maxima 'Purpurea'
Cotinus coggygria 'Royal Purple'
Photinia glabra 'Rubens' (red young leaves)
P. fraseri 'Robusta' (red young leaves)
Pieris formosa forrestii 'Wakehurst' (red young leaves)
Prunus spinosa 'Purpurea'
Rosa rubrifolia
Weigela florida 'Foliis Purpureis'
Parthenocissus henryana (climber)
Vitis vinifera 'Purpurea' (climber)

Pieris formosa forrestii

Ericaceae (heather family) S. W. China
All forms of this pieris have bronzy-red or pure red young leaves which can be as bright as a display of poinsettia flowers. An evergreen shrub of somewhat rounded habit, *forrestii* bears terminal arching clusters of white urn-shaped bell flowers in spring. Before they completely fade, the young shoots start to expand into tufts of brilliant red leaves. By mid-summer the red has faded to rich green. Partial shade retains the red leaves longest and an acid or neutral soil is essential. Although hardy in much of the temperate zone, a cold spell below 0°F (-18°C) can kill all growth to ground level.

Prunus X 'Cistena'
(purple-leaved sand cherry)

Rosaceae (rose family) garden hybrid
This striking shrub makes an erect bushy plant up to 6ft (1.8m) or so in height with bright purple-red, oval leaves. In early spring the naked branches are wreathed with white saucer-shaped blossoms like those of plum. 'Cistena' is hardy in the temperate zone and thrives in any fertile soil, whether acid or alkaline. It make an effective hedge either grown naturally or clipped to shape in late summer. Alternatively, it can be used as a specimen plant for the smaller lawn and is particularly attractive when underplanted with spring bulbs.

Calluna vulgaris 'Aurea'
(yellow-leaved heather)

Ericaceae (heather family) W. Europe
Common heather has given rise to many different forms, some in gardens, others, such as 'Aurea', as mutations in the wild. The tiny evergreen leaves are bright greenish-gold in summer with bronze-red tints in winter. In late summer and autumn terminal spikes of tiny white bell-flowers are borne. Well-developed bushes can attain 12 to 15in (30 to 38cm) in height and spread, but will be less if the shoots are cut back in spring to encourage bushy growth. It is hardy in all but the coldest parts of the temperate zone. An acid soil and a site in full sun are essential.

Lonicera nitida 'Baggessens Gold'

Caprifoliaceae (honeysuckle family) China
Dense twiggy growth and tiny polished oval leaves typify this 4 to 5ft (1 to 1.5m) tall evergreen. Its original green-leaved form is often used as a close-clipped hedge. 'Baggessen's Gold' can be used similarly but is also a useful border or accent plant among heathers. The leaves, bright golden yellow in summer, fade to greenish gold in autumn and winter. Tiny greenish flowers open in spring, followed by inconspicuous translucent purple berries. Hardy in the temperate zone, temperatures below 0°F (-18°C) may brown shoot tips. Any well-drained soil is suitable.

Berberis thunbergii 'Atropurpurea

Berberidaceae (barberry family) Japan
Usually about 6ft (1.8m) in height, this robust form of *Berberis thunbergii* is ideal for a background hedge or as a specimen plant in mixed shrub border. The round-ended leaves are borne in rosette-like clusters and when young they are a bright red-purple, maturing to a deep green-purple. In autumn they turn red before they fall. Small, pendulous, bowl-shaped yellow flowers open in spring, followed by oval, bead-like red berries. Any ordinary garden soil and a site in the sun are all that is necessary for success. It is hardy in the temperate zone.

Ilex crenata 'Golden Gem'

Aquifoliaceae (holly family) Japan
The original green-leaved species of this little evergreen holly has dark green glossy oval leaves and a compact habit and can exceed 6ft (1.8m) in height. Several good horticultural forms have been introduced to western gardens and other parts of the temperate world where it is quite hardy. 'Golden Gem' is a low-growing shrub of spreading habit, rarely exceeding 2ft (61cm) tall. The leaves are flushed with yellow which is particularly bright during the winter. Tiny insignificant white flowers are borne in spring. Any fertile garden soil is suitable and a site in sun or partial shade.

Pieris formosa forrestii

Lonicera nitida 'Baggessens Gold'

Prunus X Cistena

Berberis thunbergii 'Atropurpurea'

Calluna vulgaris 'Aurea'

Ilex crenata 'Golden Gem'

61

Variegated

Shrubs

Abutilon megapotamicum 'Variegatum'
A. X milleri
Aralia elata 'Aureovariegata'
Berberis thunbergii 'Rose Glow'
Cornus alba 'Elegantissima'
C. alternifolia 'Argentea'
C. controversa 'Variegata'
C. mas 'Variegata'
Coronilla glauca 'Variegata'
Cotoneaster horizontalis 'Variegata'
Daphne odora 'Aureomarginata'
Elaeagnus pungens 'Maculata'
Euonymus 'Silver Queen'
Fuchsia magellanica 'Versicolor'
Hebe X andersonii 'Variegata'
Hydrangea macrophylla 'Maculata'
Hypericum moserianum 'Tricolor'
Ilex aquifolium (variegated forms)
Kerria japonica 'Variegata'
Pachysandra terminalis 'Variegata'
Pieris japonica 'Variegata'
Pittosporum 'Silver Queen'
Salvia officinalis 'Icterina'
S. o. 'Tricolor'
Weigela praecox 'Variegata'

Hoheria populnea 'Variegata' (variegated lacebark)

Malvaceae (hibiscus family) New Zealand

This graceful, much-branched semi-evergreen or small tree can grow to 10ft (3m) and more in mild sheltered areas in the temperate zone. Freezing winds and more than 10° to 15°F (-5° to -8°C) of frost can seriously injure the leaves and twigs. From late summer into autumn dense clusters of ¾in (1.9cm) wide saucer-shaped white flowers are borne, often in abundance. Unlike some other variegated evergreen trees, the foliage always looks fresh and attractive. Although tolerant of alkaline soils, it does best in acid and neutral ones.

Berberis thunbergii 'Rose Glow'

Berberidaceae (barberry family)
Seldom exceeding 4ft (1.2m) tall, this unique form of the common *Berberis thunbergii* deserves a place where coloured foliage effects are required. The deciduous leaves, borne in rosette-like clusters, are purple mottled with silvery rose and pale red when young. Later, paler shades fade and the overall purple deepens. Small yellow, bowl-shaped flowers appear in spring, followed by ovoid, bead-like red berries. 'Rose Glow' thrives in sun or partial shade and in any good garden soil. It is hardy in the temperate zone, but likes a little shelter in areas where prolonged winds and frosts occur.

Elaeagnus pungens 'Maculata'

Elaeagnaceae (oleaster family) Japan
Among the hardy evergreen shrubs with variegated foliage, this one ranks high. The colour on the leathery-textured leaves is at its best when the leaves are mature, that is from autumn to spring, just when the garden needs cheering up. In autumn, dull silvery-white bell-shaped flowers, about ½in (1.2cm) long, fragrance the air. Somewhat slow-growing at first, it can eventually reach 8ft (2.4m) in height. Although best in the sun, this shrub tolerates partial shade. It grows in a wide variety of soils, providing they are well-drained and fertile, and is hardy in the temperate zone.

Ilex X altaclarensis 'Golden King' (golden holly)

Aquifoliaceae (holly family) garden hybrid

Although resembling a fine vigorous common holly (*Ilex aquifolium*), this evergreen hybrid owes much of its size and lustre to the other parent, *I. perado*, the 'Azorean holly'. Capable of reaching 10ft (3m) in height, 'Golden King' is one of the finest variegated hollies for the more sheltered temperate garden. Where prolonged spells of freezing weather occur and more than 25°F (-14°C) of frost are experienced, leaves are lost and young growth killed. It will thrive in acid and alkaline soils. This is a female form and bears berries.

Symphoricarpos orbiculatus 'Variegatus' (coral berry)

Caprifoliaceae (honeysuckle family) W. North America

A deciduous bushy, densely leafy shrub up to 6ft (1.8m). The leaves make a pleasing foil for the rose-purple berries that appear from late summer to early winter. This shrub grows in most soil types and is hardy in the temperate zone. The ordinary green-leaved species has been planted as a game covert bush in parts of Europe but is not seen as often as the white-fruited snowberries *Symphoricarpos albus* and *rivularis*. While tolerant of shade it is best in an open site where the yellow variegation is more pronounced.

Hypericum X moseranum 'Tricolor'

Guttiferae (St. John's wort family) garden hybrid

A hybrid of the well-known rose of Sharon (*H. calycinum*) and the Chinese *H. patulum*, this deciduous or semi-evergreen shrub has arching 2ft (16cm) stems clad with pale green leaves attractively variegated with splashes of white and pink. In summer, 2 to 2½in (5 to 6cm) wide golden rose-like blossoms appear with a boss of reddish stamens. Hardy in the temperate zone, it stands partial shade well and grows in a wide range of soils. To produce strong shoots and good leaf colour, it should be cut to within 6in (15cm) of the ground in early spring.

Hoheria populnea 'Variegata'

Ilex X altaclarensis 'Golden King'

Berberis thunbergii 'Rose Glow'

Symphoricarpos orbiculatus 'Variegatus'

Elaeagnus pungens 'Maculata'

Hypericum X moseranum 'Tricolor'

63

autumn & winter display

Shrubs, among all other groups of plants which are hardy in the temperate zone, can provide a remarkable display of interest, colour and beauty during the so-called dead months of late autumn to late winter. The use of evergreen foliage will brighten up an otherwise brown and leafless bed or border. Better still are the evergreens with leaves that are colourfully variegated with white, cream or bright yellow as in *Elaeagnus pungens* 'Maculata'. The dying leaves of autumn, which often turn brilliant colours, can give way to colourful stems or shining mahogany trunks as in *Prunus serrula* and *Acer griseum*. Many shrubs, from the common holly to various barberries and cotoneasters, give us colourful displays of berries in shades of red, orange, yellow, blue and purple. Perhaps most appreciated of all are the winter flowering shrubs which give a foretaste of spring.

Autumn colour foliage
Shrubs
Acer palmatum 'Osakazuki'
Amelanchier florida
Berberis thunbergii
B. wilsoniae
Cotinus americanus
Disanthus cercidifolius
Euonymus alatus
Hydrangea quercifolia
Rhododendron (azalea) molle (japonicum),
　　Knaphill and Ghent hybrids
Rhus typhina
Rosa nitida
Stephanandra incisa
Viburnum plicatum (tomentosum) 'Mariesii'
Climbers
Parthenocissus tricuspidata 'Veitchii'
Vitis amurensis
V. 'Brandt'
V. coignetiae and others

Euonymus alatus (winged spindle)

Celastraceae (spindle family) China and Japan
The Latin name *alatus* means winged, and the most distinctive feature of this bushy deciduous shrub is the broad corky wings that run down twigs and branchlets. Fairly slow-growing, this spindle can reach 6ft (1.8m) in height. The pale green leaves turn a fiery crimson in autumn. Insignificant greenish flowers in early summer give way to deep pink fruits that split to show orange seeds within. Hardy in the temperate zone, this shrub will tolerate a wide range of soil types, but it rarely colours well in chalky soils without plenty of peat or compost.

Vitis coignetiae

Vitidaceae (grape vine family) Japan, Korea
This boldly handsome, deciduous climber can produce stems 50ft (15m) long when clambering up a large tree. Grown on a wall or pergola, however, it can be kept in check by winter pruning. The large, thick-textured leaves attain 1ft (30cm) across. In autumn they turn to shades of yellow, crimson and scarlet and make a spectacular picture. Insignificant clusters of tiny flowers give rise to black-purple grapes in early autumn. This vine is hardy in the temperate zone and thrives in most fertile soils, though it colours best in acid or neutral soils.

Vaccinium corymbosum (high-bush blueberry)

Ericaceae (heather family) E. North America
Also called swamp blueberry, this large deciduous shrub can reach 6ft (1.8m) in height when happily situated. In its native USA it is cultivated mainly for the pea-sized blue-black, well-flavoured berries which ripen in late summer. It is an ornamental shrub in its own right, with bright green oval leaves that turn bronze and red in autumn, and urn-shaped, pale pink or greenish-white flowers, borne in pendant clusters in late spring. It requires a moist acid soil in a sunny site and is hardy in the temperate zone.

Sorbus hupehensis (Hupeh rowan)

Rosaceae (rose family) W. China
Strictly speaking, this Chinese Rowan or Mountain Ash is a small tree. It can however be grown in bush form and rarely exceeds 20ft (6m). The deciduous leaves are composed of 11 to 17 oval-toothed leaflets with a bluish-grey hue. In autumn they take on brilliant shades of orange and red which combine well with the white berries. The latter develop from flattened clusters of creamy flowers which are borne in late spring. The variety *S.h. obtusa* or 'Rosea' has pink fruits. *Sorbus hupehensis* is hardy in the temperate zone and will thrive in any fertile garden soil, either acid or alkaline.

Cotinus coggygria (syn. Rhus cotinus) (smoke bush)

Anacardiaceae (pistachio nut family) C. and S. Europe
This compactly rounded deciduous bush can be 8ft (2.4m) tall, but is usually less. Autumn leaves are bright yellow and red (*C.c.* 'Foliis Purpureis' leaves are flushed with red-purple throughout the summer). Tiny green flowers are borne in summer on large, plumey clusters of slender stalks clad in silky reddish hairs. A bush in flower seems covered with a red or pinky haze of smoke. Hardy in the temperate zone, soft stems may be killed during very severe winters. It thrives in a wide variety of soil types.

Mahonia X media 'Winter Sun'

Berberidaceae (barberry family) garden hybrid
There are several fine hybrids between *Mahonia lomariifolia* and *japonica*, typified by erect robust stems up to 6ft (1.8m) tall, and usually little branches clad with glossy evergreen leaves 1ft (30cm) or more long. Each leaf is composed of several sharply-toothed oval leaflets. The branch tips terminate in a rosette-like ring of leaves — an ideal background for the bright yellow flower spikes that arise from the centre in winter. It thrives best in a sheltered spot. It is hardy in the temperate zone if sheltered from freezing winds and prolonged frost.

Euonymus alatus

Sorbus hupehensis

Vitis coignetiae

Cotinus coggygria (syn. Rhus cotinus)

Vaccinium corymbosum

Mahonia X media 'Winter Sun'

Autumn berries

Shrubs

Aucuba japonica
Berberis X rubrostilla and other deciduous species
Clerodendrum trichotomum
Coriaria terminalis
C. t. 'Xanthocarpa'
Cotoneaster conspicuus 'Decorus'
C. c. X watereri 'Cornubia'
C. c. 'Highlight'
Euonymus europaeus and 'Red Cascade'
Hippophae rhamnoides
Ilex aquifolium 'J. C. Van Tol'
I. a. 'Amber' and many others
Pyracantha rogersiana
P. r. 'Flava'
Rosa moyesii 'Geranium'
Skimmia japonica (female)
Stranvaesia davidiana

Cotoneaster X watereri 'Rothschildianus'

Rosaceae (rose family) garden hybrid
Most of the many species and hybrids of *Cotoneaster* are grown for their red berries. This garden hybrid, raised at the famous Exbury Gardens, Hampshire, England, bears an abundance of creamy yellow fruits that often escape the depredations of birds. The evergreen leaves are long and oval and make a foil for the clusters of creamy summer-born flowers. Well-grown specimens can reach a height of 8 to 10ft (2.5 to 3m) with an equal spread of arching branches. This hybrid is hardy in the temperate zone, but in the colder areas many or all of the leaves will be lost in winter. Any good garden soil is suitable.

Viburnum davidii

Caprifoliaceae (honeysuckle family) W. China
This low-growing evergreen shrub, rarely exceeding 2½ft (76cm) tall, is worth growing just for its lustrous, dark green and boldly triple-veined leaves with a reddish stalk. Small flat-topped clusters of whitish flowers in mid-summer give rise to striking turquoise berries. More than one bush is required for a good crop of berries as the flowers must be cross-pollinated. Specimens from seed are either mainly male or mainly female, so nursery plants from cuttings are best. *Viburnum davidii* will grow in all fertile soils and is hardy in the temperate zone.

Skimmia japonica

Rutaceae (orange family) Japan
This woodland shrub has three facets of attraction: pleasing oval evergreen leaves, fragrant flowers and red berries. The best forms are dense and rounded, rarely exceeding 3 to 4ft (.9 to 1.2m) in height. In spring, terminal clusters of white, sometimes red-tinted, flowers appear. Later, the female plants bear bright red fruits which persist all winter. Male and female plants are needed for berries, one male to several female being adequate. The best form for flower scent is *S. j.* 'Fragrans', and 'Nymans' is good for fruit. *Skimmia* is hardy in the temperate zone and will grow in any good garden soil.

Pernettya mucronata

Ericaceae (heather family) Chile
Rarely exceeding 2ft (61cm) in height, this bushy evergreen is ideal ground cover, particularly in partial shade. Small clusters of white blossoms appear in early summer followed by marble-sized fruits from pure white to pinks and reds. Several named varieties are available. Most of these are hermaphrodites, but a better crop of berries results if several different sorts are grown together. *Pernettya* must be grown in an acid soil, and in colder parts of the temperate zone it requires a sheltered site. Prolonged temperatures of 12° to 17°F (-11°C to -8°C) will scorch and kill leaves and young shoots.

Pyracantha rogersiana 'Flava' (yellow firethorn)

Rosaceae (rose family) S. W. China
A tall spiny evergreen shrub, 'Flava' is 8ft (2.5m) or more tall, with glossy, toothed, narrow leaves that widen towards the tip. During early summer, flattened clusters of small creamy flowers are borne in profusion. These are followed by an equal abundance of bright yellow berries that last well into the winter if they are not eaten by the birds. Although this is a hardy shrub in the temperate zone which can be grown in beds and borders and as a hedge, it is particularly effective against a wall. Any good garden soil, acid or alkaline, is suitable.

Sorbus hupehensis (hupeh rowan)

Rosaceae (rose family) W. China
Strictly speaking this *Sorbus* is of tree form, but it can be grown as a large shrub and rarely grows above 15 to 20ft (4.5 to 6.1m). The ash-like leaves are composed of several toothed, bluish-green, oval leaflets. These are barely expanded when the creamy white flowers are borne in late spring. The usually profuse berries are white and frequently pink-tinged and hang long after the leaves have fallen, birds permitting. The leaves usually take on shades of glowing red in autumn. This rowan is hardy in the temperate zone and will thrive in any good garden soil.

Cotoneaster X 'Rothschildianus'

Pernettya mucronata

Viburnum davidii

Pyracantha rogersiana 'Flava'

Skimmia japonica

Sorbus hupehensis

67

Winter display—flowers and stems
Shrubs

Abeliophyllum distichum
Acer davidii
A. palmatum 'Senkaki'
A. pennsylvanicum
Arbutus X andrachnoides
A. unedo
Betula ermanii
B. papyrifera
Camellia japonica
C. saluenensis
C. sasanqua
C. X Williamsii
Chimonanthus praecox
Clematis calycina
Cornus alba 'Sibirica'
Cornus mas
C. stolonifera 'Flaviramea'
Corylus avellana 'Contorta'
Daphne laureola
D. mezereum
Edgworthia papyrifera
Erica arborea alpina
E. carnea
E. X darleyensis
E. mediterranea (erigena)
Forsythia giraldiana
Garrya elliptica
Hamamelis X intermedia
H. japonica
H. mollis
Jasminum nudiflorum
Lonicera fragrantissima
L. X standishii
Mahonia bealei
M. lomariifolia
Parottia persica
Prunus davidiana
P. maackii
P. serrula
P. serrulata semperflorens
P. subhirtella 'Autumnalis'
Rhododendron arboreum
R. barbatum
R. 'Christmas Cheer'
R. 'Cornubia'
R. mucronulatum
R. X nobleanum
R. X praecox
R. stewartianum
Rosa omeiensis
R. pteracantha
Salix alba 'Chermesina'
S. caprea
S. daphnoides
S. matsudana 'Tortuosa'
Sarcococca hookeriana digyna
S. humilis
S. ruscifolia
Stachyurus praecox
Viburnum x bodnantense
V. farreri
V. grandiflorum
V. tinus

Viburnum tinus
(laurustinus)

Caprifoliaceae (honeysuckle family)
Mediterranean to S.E. Europe
This familiar evergreen tends to be overlooked in the modern garden, even though there are several fine forms superior to the original wild plant. It forms a rounded bush up to 8ft (2.4m) or so and sometimes assumes the form of a small tree. From autumn through to spring, wide flattened heads of small white blossoms expand in succession, sometimes followed by steely-blue fruits. Any ordinary soil that is well-drained is suitable and the site can be in sun or partial shade. It is hardy in all but the coldest parts of the temperate zone.

Mahonia lomariifolia

Berberidaceae (barberry family) China and Formosa (Taiwan)
This evergreen shrub can attain 8 to 10ft (2.4 to 3m) in height in a site sheltered from freezing winds. Temperatures below 10°F (-12°C) can kill it above ground level. The dark, lustrous leaves are composed of 15 to 19 pairs of holly-like leaflets. From late autumn into winter, a fountain-like cluster of flower spikes erupt from each stem. Individual spikes can be 10in (25cm) long and bear many small, rich yellow, bell-like blossoms. A soil enriched with leaf-mould, peat or compost and a partially shaded site, preferably beneath trees, gives the best results.

Daphne mezereum
(mezereon)

Thymelaeaceae (daphne family) Europe to Siberia
In temperate countries where the winters are intermittently mild, this charming deciduous daphne opens its first blossoms early in winter. The white or red-purple flower clusters distil a sweet and powerful fragrance for yards around. 'Grandiflora', syn. 'Autumnalis', has larger blossoms and begins to flower in the autumn. Any well-drained soil is suitable and a site in partial shade or full sun. It is hardy in the temperate region. This daphne is sometimes short-lived in gardens, but is very easily raised from seeds.

Cornus alba 'Sibirica'
(Westonbirt dogwood)

Cornaceae (dogwood family) Siberia to Korea
The original *Cornus alba* (red-barked dogwood) forms a suckering thicket of erect, sparse branched stems up to 6ft (1.8m) tall. The leaves fall in autumn leaving lacquer-red twigs which glow brightly on sunny winter days. The colouring is restricted to one-year-old twigs, so it is best to cut back the bushes each spring. In summer, small creamy flower heads appear, then whitish berries. *C. alba* 'Sibirica' is less vigorous and its twigs a more brilliant crimson. It is hardy in the temperate zone and thrives in any fertile soil.

Rubus biflorus
(whitewashed bramble)

Rosaceae (rose family) Himalaya
Thriving in partial shade or sun, this ornamental bramble provides an unusual winter display. After the leaves fall in autumn, the cane-like stems appear to be painted with a waxy blue-white whitewash. In shade the stems can exceed 6ft (1.8m) in height, but they are usually less in sun. The leaves are composed of several narrowly oval leaflets. In summer, small white flowers appear in few-flowered terminal clusters, followed by fruits like yellow raspberries. These are edible, but not very tasty. *Rubus biflorus* is hardy in the temperate zone and likes any well-drained, moderately fertile soil.

Hamamelis mollis
(Chinese witch hazel)

Hamamelidaceae (witch hazel family) China
This superb mid-winter performer can grow to 10ft (3m) in height, but it takes several years to reach half this. The leaves, covered with short soft hairs, turn a rich yellow in autumn. It blooms from December to February or later. The golden-yellow flower clusters give off a strong sweet fragrance. It needs a neutral to acid soil, preferably in the shelter of trees but not too densely shaded. It is hardy in the temperate zone, but only flowers in winter if the temperature goes above 40°F to 45°F (4° to 7°C) for a week or so.

Viburnum tinus

Cornus alba 'Sibirica'

Mahonia lomariifolia

Rubus biflorus

Daphne mezereum

Hamamelis mollis

69

beautiful flowers

For those gardeners who are not after a massed display of flowers but prefer the form and colouring of individual flowers, shrubs have much to offer. Among the hordes of rhododendrons species and hybrids can be found those which provide superb masses of colour and blossoms of individual beauty. Camellias and magnolias are obvious candidates for the individual beauty stakes. Magnolia in particular has several species and hybrids that produce large blossoms of classic goblet form in subtle shades of white, pink and crimson purple. We should not be blinded by sheer size. Many quite small flowers have great beauty when viewed closely. Most noteworthy in this category is *Kalmia latifolia*, each ¾in (19mm) wide blossom resembling an almost translucent pink lampshade by a master designer.

Shrubs

Abutilon magapotamicum
A. vitifolium
Camellia japonica, C. recticulata, C. sasanqua,
   C. X williamsii
Campsis radicans (climber)
Cantua buxifolia
Carpenteria californica
Cistus ladanifer, C. palhinhae, C. X purpureus
Clematis x jackmanii, C. macropetala, C. tangutica,
   C. viticella (all climbers)
Cornus florida, C. nuttallii
Crinodendron hookerianum
Datura suaveolens
Desfontainea spinosa
Eucryphia x nymansensis
Fuchsia hybrids (many vars.)
Gordonia lasianthus
Hibiscus sinosyriacus
Hydrangea macrophylla (many vars.)
Hypericum 'Hidcote', H. 'Rowallane'
Kalimia latifolia
Lapageria rosea (climber)
Magnolia denudata, M. grandifiora, M. sinensis,
   M. X soulangiana, M. wilsonii.
Michelia doltsopa
Paeonia suffruticosa (many vars.)
Passiflora caerulea (climber)
Philesia magellanica
Punica granatum
Rhododendron albrechtii, R. campanulatum,
   R. cinnabarinum, R. griffithianum,
   R. nuttallii, R. sinogrande, R. thomsonii,
   R. many hybrid vars.
Rubus X tridel
Styrax obassia
Tibouchina urvilleana

Rosa X 'Apricot Silk'

Rosaceae (rose family) garden hybrid
This fairly new hybrid tea rose forms a vigorous upright bush, reaching 3 to 4ft (.9 to 1.2m) with moderate pruning. The rich green foliage is composed of 3 to 5 or more oval leaflets. From summer to autumn a succession of shapely blooms, with a slight fragrance, unfold from long slender buds. It is suitable for bedding or for cut flowers and lasts well in water. It should be pruned each spring by cutting back the previous season's growth to about 4in (10cm). A fertile, moist but well-drained soil is needed for best results, plus a sunny site. It is hardy in all but the coldest parts of the temperate zone.

Fuchsia 'Queen Mary'

Onagraceae (fuchsia family)
Although there are a wealth of fine new fuchsia hybrids, several of the old ones, like 'Queen Mary', retain their popularity. This deciduous shrub grows up to 4ft (1.2m) in height. The flowers have a pale pink tube with white-tipped pink sepals and pink petals which age to rosy-purple. 'Queen Mary' thrives in the open garden only in the warmest areas of the temperate zone and is not hardy unless protected with a mound of weathered ashes, sand or bracken. It makes a fine patio plant when grown in a large pot and blooms from summer to autumn. Any good potting compost or garden soil is suitable.

Camellia japonica 'Shiro-botan'

Theaceae (tea-tree family) Japan, China
Many garden forms of *Camellia japonica* have come out of China and Japan since the first one in 1739. 'Shiro-botan, comes from Japan and forms a vigorous evergreen bush up to 6ft (1.8m). The dark green, polished, elliptic leaves combine splendidly with the large, white, semi-double blossoms which expand from late winter to spring. The bush itself is hardy in the temperate zone, but the flowers can be browned by frost. A neutral to acid soil, preferably enriched with leaf-mould or peat, is necessary for success. A site beneath trees or against a sheltered wall is ideal.

Magnolia X soulangiana

Magnoliaceae (magnolia family)
This hardy deciduous magnolia grows up to 15ft (4.6m) tall. Tolerating a wide range of soil types it provides a regular display of beautiful flowers each spring. Its beauty is on two levels; that of a massed display from a distance and that of the individual blossom. The firm, broad petals overlap to create a chalice-shaped bloom of great aesthetic appeai. There are several fine forms of this magnolia which range from white to a rich red-purple. 'Alba Superba' is one of the best white forms, with fragrant blooms, and the rich rosy-purple 'Rustica Rubra' is recommended among the darker kinds.

Camellia reticulata 'Buddha'

Theaceae (tea-tree family) W. China
Camellia reticulata forms an erect bush up to 10ft (3m) tall under ideal conditions, though is easily maintained at half this height if grown in pots or tubs. The oval leaves are evergreen and tapered to a point. In their axils are borne large rose-like blooms of semi-double form. They open in early spring or even late winter in warm areas. This camellia is hardy outside only in the warmer parts of the temperate zone and flower buds are killed by moderate frosts. It needs a neutral to acid soil, preferably enriched with peat or lime-free leaf-mould.

Hypericum patulum forrestii

Guttiferae (St. John's wort family)
China, Assam, Burma
Also called *H. p.henryi*, this St John's wort is a species in its own right and should be called *H. forrestii*. It forms a compact rounded, deciduous bush about 3ft (.9m) tall. The bright yellow bowl-shaped blossoms are 2 to 2½in (5 to 6.3cm) across and open in abundance during the summer with a lesser display into the autumn. This shrub is hardy in the temperate zone, though soft young shoot tips may be damaged or killed during spells of freezing winds. It will thrive in any good garden soil providing it is not waterlogged.

Rosa X 'Apricot Silk'

Magnolia X soulangiana

Fuchsia 'Queen Mary'

Camellia reticulata 'Buddha'

Camellia japonica 'Shiro-botan'

Hypericum patulum forrestii

71

rhodo- dendrons & azaleas

For the lucky gardener who has neutral to acid soil, rhododendrons have much to offer. Among the 600-odd species and their numerous hybrids and forms, it is possible to plan a garden with year-round interest without bringing in a plant from any other genus. Not that this is necessarily desirable, but it shows how versatile rhododendrons are. In leaf size they can range from under $\frac{1}{2}$in (1.27cm) to 2ft (61cm) long and in overall height from mat-forming kinds to trees 40ft (12m) or more tall. Some species have very decorative foliage; rich green and glossy and boldly veined or clothed in tawny or rust red hairs. Flower form is equally variable, some species having tiny starry blossoms, others bearing massive waxy bells. Taking the genus as a whole, fragrance is not a common feature, but some sorts have deliciously fragrant blossoms, whilst others have sweetly or pungently aromatic leaves. Although all of them (with a very few exceptions) must have acid soil, there are many to choose from that thrive in full sun to partial shade to the permanent, but dappled, shade of trees. Thus it can be clearly seen that by choosing carefully, a garden of varied shapes, textures and floral effect can be produced.

Nowadays, plant taxonomists place all the various sorts of azalea into the genus *Rhododendron*. Azaleas were originally placed in a genus of their own on the basis of the number of stamens in each flower. Azaleas have 5 stamens, whereas rhododendrons have 10. This small botanical character is no longer considered sufficiently important to separate at the generic level.

Rhododendron X 'Ima-shojo' (syn 'Christmas Cheer')

Ericaceae (heather family) garden hybrid
A Japanese Kurume azalea hybrid, 'Ima-shojo' is often listed as 'Christmas Cheer'. It forms a semi-evergreen compact, rounded bush about 3 to 4ft (.9 to 1.2m) in height and slightly more in girth. In spring, each of the slender, crowded twigs bears $1\frac{1}{4}$in (3cm) wide funnel-shaped flowers which appear semi-double, as the calyx is enlarged and coloured like the petals. A site beneath well-spaced trees is best, but sunnier positions are suitable if protected from freezing winds. An acid soil is necessary. It is hardy in all but the coldest parts of the temperate zone.

Rhododendron X 'Hatsugiri'

Ericaceae (heather family) garden hybrid from Japan
'Hatsugiri' is a typical member of the Japanese dwarf hybrid group known as Kurume azaleas. All are rounded and compact with slender twigs and semi-evergreen leaves. They range from 2 to 4ft (61 to 122cm) in height. 'Hatsugiri' is a dwarf of rounded, spreading outline. In spring it is smothered with eye-catching crimson blossoms. A site beneath well-spaced trees is best, but sunnier sites are suitable if sheltered from freezing winds. An acid soil that does not dry out too rapidly is essential. It is hardy in all but the coldest parts of the temperate zone.

Rhododendron X 'Frome'

Ericaceae (heather family) garden hybrid
'Frome' is a fine representative of the deciduous azalea group known as Knap Hill. Anthony Waterer originated this group by crossing the Ghent azaleas with *Rhododendron calendulaceum, occidentale* and *japonicum (syn. molle)*. They form compact bushes 4 to 6ft (1.2 to 1.8m) tall with oval pale green, often hairy leaves. In late spring, 'Frome' produces an abundance of saffron-yellow, widely funnel-shaped blooms with a bright orange-red suffusion in the throat. A site in sun or partial shade is suitable and an acid soil that does not dry out excessively is essential. It is hardy in the temperate zone.

Rhododendron X 'Mary Swaythling'

Ericaceae (heather family) garden hybrid
This attractive evergreen was raised at Chilworth Manor, Southampton, England, in the early 1920's. Its parents were the clear yellow *R. campylocarpum* and the pale rose-purple *R. fortunei*. 'Mary Swaythling' favours the first with sulphur-yellow, bell-shaped flowers in late spring. It forms a shapely bush up to 7ft (2m) tall with smooth oval leaves. An acid soil rich in humus is required for success with, preferably, the dappled light from well-spaced trees. It is generally hardy in the temperate zone, though temperatures below 0°F (-18°C) may damage the buds exposed on the branches all winter.

Rhododendron X 'Irene Koster'

Ericaceae (heather family) garden hybrid
This deciduous hybrid Azalea is characteristic of the Occidentale Hybrid group. 'Irene Koster' makes a compact bush up to 6ft (1.8m) tall, though it takes several years to attain this height. The pale green leaves are oval and are only partly expanded when the terminal trusses of flowers appear in late spring. Each is creamy-white, suffused and lined with pink and bearing a yellow blotch within. Although it grows well in the dappled light of open woodland, it flowers more profusely in a sunny site. An acid soil that does not dry out excessively is essential. It is hardy in the temperate zone.

Rhododendron recticulatum

Ericaceae (heather family) Japan
This species belongs to the azalea section of the genus *Rhododendron* and is deciduous. The broadly oval, pale green leaves bear russet hairs when young and retain shorter hairs on the underside when mature. They are borne on a slender-twigged bush that reaches 7ft (2m) in height. Before the leaves unfurl in spring, bright rose-purple flowers garland all the stem tips. These blossoms are about $1\frac{1}{2}$in (3.8cm) across and widely funnel-shaped. A moderately sunny site gives the most prolific flowering, but partial shade is also suitable. An acid soil is essential. It is hardy in the temperate zone.

Rhododendron X 'Mrs P. D. Williams'

Ericaceae (heather family) garden hybrid

Grown in a sheltered, moderately sunny position, this evergreen hybrid is one of the most prolific bloomers of all rhododendrons. In full bloom in early summer, hardly a leaf can be seen. The blossoms are ivory-white, with a large sienna blotch on the upper petals. 'Mrs P. D. Williams' is not fully hardy in the temperate zone; temperatures below 0°F (-18°C) are likely to kill the buds, which are on the twigs all winter. Depending on the shadiness of the site, this hybrid can range from 3 to 5ft (.9 to 1.5m) or more in height. It needs an acid soil that does not dry out excessively.

Rhododendron X 'Professor Hugo de Vries'

Ericaceae (heather family) garden hybrid

This fine hybrid evergreen *Rhododendron* was produced by crossing the legendary 'Pink Pearl' with 'Doncaster'. 'Professor Hugo de Vries' forms a large shrub 7ft (2m) and more in height. It is of compact growth with rich green narrowly oval leaves. The large terminal flower clusters which appear from late spring to early summer are compact and conical. The flower buds are a rich pink, opening to lilac-rose, and bear a flash of deep reddish markings in the throat. Acid soil is necessary for success and a site in sun or partial shade. It is hardy in temperate zone.

Rhododendron thomsonii

Ericaceae (heather family) Sikkim, Nepal, Bhutan, Tibet

This fine evergreen was brought from the Himalayas in 1849. It grows at a moderate pace and eventually forms a bush 6 to 8ft (1.8 to 2.4m) high and wide. Mature leaves are rounded to oval and glossy rich green with pale or white undersides. When young, they are bright blue-green with an almost metallic lustre. Large deep-crimson waxy-textured bell-flowers provide an eye-catching spring display. It fares best in the dappled shade of light woodland but grows in sun if the site is not dry and windy. An acid soil is essential. It is hardy in the temperate zone.

Rhododendron augustinii

Ericaceae (heather family) Tibet and N. China

Capable of reaching 10ft (3m) in height, this *Rhododendron* evergreen is slow-growing and takes several years to attain half this size. It has narrow, pointed leaves on slender well-branched stems, which in spring are almost obscured by a profusion of funnel-shaped 2in (5cm)-wide blossoms of lavender-blue or mauve with chrome-yellow markings. Raised from seeds, the flower colourings can be variable. It is advisable to obtain a named form such as 'Electra' or *R.a. chasmanthum*. It requires an acid soil and is hardy in the temperate zone.

Rhododendron X 'Susan'

Ericaceae (heather family) garden hybrid

Arising as a cross between *campanulatum* from the Himalayas and *fortunei* from China — 'Susan' is one of the best evergreen hybrids in its class, on whom the Royal Horticultural Society has bestowed an Award of Merit, First Class Certificate and an Award of Garden Merit (1969). It forms a tall bush up to 10ft (3m) or so, but takes a number of years to attain this height. Large trusses of blue-mauve, bell-shaped blossoms with purple spotting open in spring. It is hardy in the temperate zone and does best in light woodland. A sunnier site is tolerated but the blooms fade more rapidly.

Rhododendron arboreum 'Roseum'

Ericaceae (heather family) Himalayas: Kashmir to Bhutan

In its native mountains, this fine deciduous species grows up to 40ft (12m) tall, but it is relatively slow-growing and takes several years to reach a quarter this size. The dark leaves are narrow, ovate and an ideal background for the rich pink globular flower heads which are abundant on mature plants. Hardy in the temperate zone, the flowers which open from early to mid-spring are liable to frost damage. The original *R. arboreum* varies in colour from white ('Album') to deep red with an extra-deep one known as 'Blood Red'. An acid soil is essential.

Rhododendron X 'Ima-shojo'

Rhododendron X 'Mary Swaythling'

Rhododendron X 'Hatsugiri'

Rhododendron X 'Irene Koster'

Rhododendron X 'Frome'

Rhododendron reticulatum

Rhododendron X 'Mrs. P. D. Williams'

Rhododendron X 'Professor Hugo de Vries'

Rhododendron thomsonii

Rhododendron augustinii

Rhododendron X 'Susan'

Rhododendron arboreum 'Roseum'

Rhododendrons and ericas are among the plants in this well-planned garden section. Note the careful grading of the plants into foreground, middle distance and background. Also note the upright lines of the conifer used as a focal point amidst the low-growing foreground shrubs.

clematis

Setting aside a handful of herbaceous perennial species, the genus *Clematis* comprises well over 200 species of woody climbers. Their mode of climbing is interesting, as the midrib of each compound leaf, acting as a tendril, twines around the nearest support. Although most clematis are climbers, their foliage and, particularly, their flowers vary widely in size and shape. The popular garden hybrids bear flat circular flowers several inches across and are composed of 6 to 8 petal-like sepals. Among the species there are flowers like stars, bells, urns and lanterns and in colours that range from white, pink, red, purple, lavender to yellow. Some of these species have the added attraction of decorative globular seed heads made up of tiny oval nutlets each with a long feathery tail of silky hairs. Any well-drained soil is suitable, from acid to alkaline. It should however be fertile and well-enriched with leaf-mould, compost, manure or peat. If possible the rooting area should be in the shade of low shrubs. Some means of support is necessary and this can be an arbor, trellis on a wall or the branches of an old or dead tree. The latter is particularly effective.

Clematis macropetala
(Chinese atragene)
Ranunculaceae (buttercup family) China and Siberia

The Atragene group of clematis are distinct in having narrow slender-pointed petal-like sepals, and some of the stamens are modified to small petals. Each blossom is borne solitarily in the axil of a leaf and is pendulous. The deciduous leaves are composed of several narrow mid-green leaflets carried on wiry stems that can reach 8 to 10ft (2.4 to 3m) in length. It flowers in late spring and summer. Any fertile soil in sun or partial shade is suitable, providing the site does not dry out excessively.

Clematis X 'Nelly Moser'
Ranunculaceae (buttercup family)

'Nelly Moser' is one of the very large-flowered clematis with broad wheel-like flowers about 6in (15cm) across. They are borne in profusion in early summer with a lesser display in autumn. 'Nelly Moser' can reach 15ft (4.5m) in height. It is deciduous and hardy in the temperate zone and tolerates a wide range of soils, providing they are well-drained. It thrives best if the root area is in the shade of low shrubs and looks well growing over an old tree. Tending to fade in strong sunlight, it is an ideal subject for a wall in the shade where its flowers retain their colouring without bleaching.

Clematis chrysocoma
Ranunculaceae (buttercup family) W. China

This fast-growing deciduous climber looks superb growing through an old tree or over a large arbour. Given a tall enough support, it can attain 30 to 40ft (9 to 12m), but can be kept in check by pinching out the climbing shoots during the summer. In late spring and early summer 2 to 2½in (5 to 6cm) wide four-petalled blossoms of soft pink are borne in profusion, followed by small seed clusters with silky hairy tails. This fine clematis is hardy in the temperate zone and will thrive in any fertile soil. Sandy or thin chalky soils should be enriched with leaf-mould or peat.

Clematis florida 'Sieboldii'
Ranunculaceae (buttercup family) Japan

This distinctive clematis, sometimes listed as *C. florida bicolor*, has the charm and some of the appearance of a passion flower (*Passiflora*). The 3 to 4in (7.6 to 10cm) wide blooms open green-tinted and mature white. The flowering period is from late spring to summer, sometimes with further blossoms in autumn. This deciduous or semi-evergreen climber is hardy in the temperate zone and can be grown on trees, pergolas, trellises and walls where it can attain 10ft (3m) in height. It likes its roots area in the shade and will grow on alkaline and acid soils providing they are well-drained and fertile.

Clematis X jackmanii 'Etoile Violette'
Ranunculaceae (buttercup family)

This large-flowered, deciduous, hybrid clematis was originated in 1860 by C. Jackman and has given rise to many superb garden varieties. 'Etoile Violette' has glowing violet-purple flowers, about 4in (10cm) across, that open during the summer. This clematis is hardy in the temperate zone and tolerant of a wide range of soil types if they are well-drained. It does best if the root area is in the shade of low shrubs and can be most effective climbing up an old tree. Grown on a wall it is best pruned back to within 1ft (30cm) of the ground in early spring.

Clematis X 'Hagley Hybrid'
Ranunculaceae (Buttercup family) garden hybrid

This large hybrid clematis is of moderate vigour, rarely exceeding 6ft (1.8m) in height. The stalks of the deciduous leaves act as tendrils when they come in contact with supporting wires or twigs. 'Hagley Hybrid' flowers profusely around midsummer with a lesser display to autumn. Any moisture-retentive but well-drained soil is suitable. It should be planted where at least the tops of stems can reach sunlight, and looks effective growing through an old apple tree. Alternatively plant against a sunny wall or over a pergola. It is hardy in the temperate region.

Clematis macropetala

Clematis florida 'Sieboldii'

Clematis X 'Nelly Moser'

Clematis X jackmanii 'Etoile Violette'

Clematis chrysocoma

Clematis X 'Hagley Hybrid'

79

wall shrubs & climbers

All too little use is made of walls as a home for plants. The objections that are often raised are that wall plants make the house dirty, encourage insects that find their way indoors and damage the structure. None of these objections are valid in any serious sense, though there may be an extra woodlouse or earwig above what can be normally expected. In their favour, wall shrub and climbers, if grown in quantity, can help to keep the house warmer and drier and protect the walls from weathering. They also marry the house to the garden and can provide year-round interest in foliage, flower and fruit. And for the bird lover, there is the bonus that well-grown wall shrubs make fine nesting sites. It is important to realize that narrow borders next to walls are often surpringly dry, either because they are over-shadowed by the eaves or are in the lee of rain-bearing winds. So do not plant too close to the wall and make sure the young plants do not want for water until they are well-established.

Shrubs

Actinidia chinensis
A. kolomikta
Akebia quinata
Aristolochia sipho
Azara microphylla
Billardiera longiflora
Buddleia colvilei
B. crispa
Callistemon salignus
C. speciosus
Camellia japonica in variety
C. reticulata in variety
C. sasanqua in variety
C. X williamsii in variety
Campsis (Tecoma) grandiflora
C. (Tecoma) radicans
Carpenteria californica
Ceanothus all kinds particularly:-
Ceanothus 'Burkwoodii'
C. 'Delight'
C. dentatus
C. 'Gloire de Versailles'
C. Thrysiflorus
Celastrus orbiculatus
Clematis—most species and hybrids
Clianthus puniceus

Clematis tangutica

Ranunculaceae (buttercup family) N.W. China, Mongolia
Fast-growing and elegant, this decidous clematis is worth growing for its foliage alone. Each leaf is divided into sea-green leaflets, creating a light, fern-like effect. From late summer to late autumn, a succession of pendant bright yellow flowers appear. These, unlike the usual hybrid clematis, have four pointed, petal-like sepals which form an angular bell of great charm. They are followed by globular seed heads with long, silky, hairy tails. Any fertile garden soil is suitable and reasonable sun assures blooming. It is hardy in the temperate zone.

Camellia reticulata 'Captain Rawes'

Theaceae (tea tree family) W. China
Camellia reticulata forms a tall bush up to 10ft (3m) with dark, leathery, pointed oval evergreen leaves. In late winter and early spring, large rose-red to carmine flowers expand. As the buds unfurl, each blossom has a rather funnel-like form, but finally opens out flat to reveal the cluster of extra petals within. A fertile acid to neutral soil is necessary and a sheltered wall in the colder parts of the temperate zone. Flower buds and shoot tips may be killed in temperatures below 10°F (-12°C). It makes a fine plant for the cool or cold greenhouse, where it will flower earlier.

Actinidia chinensis (Chinese gooseberry or Kiwi fruit)

Actinidiaceae (actinidia family) China
A vigorous deciduous climber, the Chinese gooseberry is an ideal subject for covering unsightly walls and buildings and looks well over an old or dead tree. In late summer, fragrant clusters of bowl-shaped creamy-white flowers appear. These are followed by oval, hairy greenish fruits with a gooseberry-like flavour. There are several named varieties grown especially for fruit. The picture shows a New Zealand kind known as 'Abbot's'. Any fertile soil is suitable and a sunny site is preferred. It is hardy in all but the coldest parts of the temperate zone.

Feijoa sellowiana (pineapple gauva)

Myrtaceae (eucalyptus family) S. South America
The broadly oval evergreen leaves of this tender 6 to 10ft (1.8 to 3m) shrub are thick, dark green and prominently veined above and white-felted beneath. In summer, white and crimson flowers appear. The curiously bunched petals are fleshy and edible with an aromatic flavour. Ovoid, berry-like fruits, about 2½in (6.3cm) long and green-tinged red, appear if the summers are long and hot. A sheltered wall is required in all but the warmest areas and severe damage can result if the temperature drops to 10°F (-12°C) or below. Any fertile soil is suitable.

Solanum crispum (potato vine)

Solanaceae (potato family) Chile
Often called a climber this ally of the potato is more correctly a scrambling shrub, In the wild, it scrambles through other shrubs or sprawls over the ground. In gardens it is best trained to a sunny but sheltered wall, where it can attain 10ft (3m) in height. The deciduous rich green leaves go well with the clusters of blue-purple potato-like blossoms that appear in summer and autumn. Any fertile well-drained soil is suitable. It is not reliably hardy in the temperate zone, but will survive 20°F (-11°C) of frost on a wall. Even if killed to ground level it usually sprouts again in spring.

Rosa bracteata (Macartney rose)

Rosaceae (rose family) China
This evergreen rose is only hardy in more sheltered parts of the temperate zone and can suffer defoliation and death of young shoots as temperatures drop close to 0°F (-18°C). In summer, pure-white single lemon-scented blossoms, 3 to 4in (7 to 10cm) across, appear. A distinctive feature is the ring of leaf-like bracts beneath each flower. Globular orange-red hips follow the flowers. *Rosa bracteata* forms a large loose shrub with scrambling stems up to 8ft (2.5m). Except in the mildest areas, it is best trained on a sheltered wall facing a sunny aspect. Any fertile soil is suitable.

Clematis tangutica

Feijoa sellowiana

Camellia reticulata 'Captain Rawes'

Solanum crispum

Actinidia chinensis

Rosa bracteata

81

Ceanothus impressus
(Californian lilac)

Rhamnaceae (buckthorn family) W. USA

This charming and profusely blooming shrub comes from California. Of bushy habit, it can reach 8ft (2.5m) or more when trained to a wall. The tiny, neatly rounded evergreen leaves are distinctive, with deeply impressed veins and a finely-toothed and hairy margin. In spring, every slender twig is wreathed in numerous small powder-puff clusters of minute deep-blue flowers. Any well-drained soil is suitable, but the site must be both sheltered and sunny for best results. Freezing winds and temperatures below 10°F (-12°C) can cause severe damage to young stems.

Kerria japonica 'Pleniflora' (bachelor's buttons)

Rosaceae (rose family) Japan and China
Introduced from China in 1804 this suckering, deciduous shrub soon became a favourite in western gardens. It is hardy in the temperate zone and looks particularly well on a red brick wall as the green stems lend themselves to training out flat. In good soil these stems can attain 7ft (2.1m) in height but will be less in poorer, drier soils. In late spring there are many bright yellow, double, pompon-like blossoms. A further sprinkling of blooms can appear from summer to autumn. Any well-drained soil is suitable and the wall can face in any direction.

Wisteria sinensis (Chinese wisteria)

Leguminosae (pea family) China
One of the most popular climbing plants, *Wisteria* is named after Caspar Wistar, a 19th-Century American professor. Happily situated, the deciduous *W. sinensis* can attain 40ft (12m) in length and looks superb growing through an old tree. Alternatively it should be grown over arbours or on walls. In spring, mauve to lilac pea-flowers are borne in pendant clusters up to 1ft (30cm) long. They appear while the leaves are very young and thus create a greater impact. *Wisteria* grows in any fertile soil, but thin chalky ones should be enriched with leaf-mould or rotted manure. It is hardy in the temperate zone.

Chaenomeles X superba
(Japonica or Japanese quince)

Rosaceae (rose family) garden hybrid
The true 'Japonica' of western gardens is *Chaenomeles japonica*, a wild species from the mountains of Japan. It has given way in latter years to its hybrid *C. x superba*, also called Japonica or Japanese quince. Both are deciduous, twiggy shrubs from 3 to 5ft (.9 to 1.5m) when trained flat on walls. From early spring to early summer and sometimes in late autumn and winter, bowl-shaped flowers appear either with the leaves or on naked twigs. The many varieties have flowers from white to deep crimson. It is hardy in the temperate zone and thrives in any well-drained soil.

Hedera helix 'Gold Heart' (syn. Jubilee)

Araliaceae (ivy family) garden origin
Formerly known as 'Jubilee' and sometimes still listed as such, 'Gold Heart' is one of the most popular of the small-leaved ivies. The self-clinging erect-growing stems bear glossy, dark-green evergreen leaves of three main pointed lobes with a prominent splash of gold in the centre. Any well-drained soil is suitable, either acid or alkaline. Any aspect in sun or shade will do, but the bright foliage makes this shrub particularly suitable for a shaded site. It should be sheltered from prolonged freezing winds, which can scorch the leaves. Temperatures below 0°F (-18°C) can also kill young shoots.

Abutilon megapotamicum
(weeping Chinese lantern)

Malvaceae (hibiscus family) Brazil
This striking semi-evergreen can be grown outside on sheltered sunny walls only in the milder parts of the temperate zone. Temperatures below 20°F (-7°C) can severely damage or kill the shoots. Happily situated, it can reach 6ft (1.8cm) or more when trained out flat. In the axils of each of the upper leaves slender wiry stalks carry quaint pendulous lantern-shaped flowers during summer and autumn. Any well-drained fertile soil that does not dry out is suitable. In the colder areas this *Abutilon* makes a good pot or tub plant for the summer patio.

Ceanothus impressus

Chaenomeles X superba

Kerria japonica 'Pleniflora'

Hedera helix 'Gold Heart'

Wisteria sinensis

Abutilon megapotamicum

83

tree-like shrubs

There is no definite rule that decides the dividing line between a large shrub and small tree. In an arbitrary way one can say that when a shrub exceeds 15ft (4.5m) it becomes a tree. In general this works well enough, providing form is also taken into account. A recognizable tree should have a clearly marked trunk with the lowest branch at least 4ft (1.2m) above the ground. On the other hand many large trees branch at, or very close to, the ground. Sheer size is the criterion here. The 15ft (4.6m) limit is used, whether the plant is branched below, at, or well above ground level. It must be noted however that in a particularly rich soil or · when old, some of the recommended species may exceed this height.

Shrubs
Aralia chinensis
A. spinosa
Cercis siliquastrum
Cotoneaster 'Cornubia'
C. 'Rothschildianus'
C. franchetii sternianus
Cornus kousa chinensis
C. nuttallii
Eucalyptus niphophila
E. gunnii and others
Eucryphia X nymansensis 'Nymansay'
Hydrangea sargentiana
Ilex aquifolium
I. altaclarensis
Magnolia denudata
M. grandiflora
M. kobus
M. X soulangiana salicifolia
M. sprengeri
Myrtus apiculata (luma)
Olea europaea
Prunus incisa
Sophora tetraptera 'Grandiflora'
Stewartia sinensis
Styrax japonica
S. obassia
Trachycarpus fortunei (excelsa)

Conifers
Chamaecyparis lawsoniana 'Allumii'
C. l. 'Fletcheri'
C. l. 'Pembury Blue'
C. l. 'Stewartii'
Cupressus glabra 'Pyramidalis'
Thuya plicata 'Zebrina'
T. p. 'Semperaurescens'
Cryptomeria japonica 'Elegans'
Juniperus virginiana 'Manhattan Blue'

Cornus kousa chinensis (Chinese flowering dogwood)

Cornaceae (dogwood family)

This large spreading shrub can attain 10ft (3m), but is usually less in gardens. The oval, deciduous leaves are prominently veined and colour bronze and crimson in autumn. In late spring or early summer the arching stems are covered with large pure-white 'flowers'. Each so-called flower is a small rounded cluster of insignificant blossoms surrounded by four petal-like leaves or bracts. This dogwood is hardy in the temperate zone but thrives best in a sheltered spot and does well in light woodland. It needs neutral or acid soil enriched with peat or leaf-mould.

Cotinus americanus (syn. Rhus cotinoides) (American smoke tree)

Anacardiaceae (pistachio nut family) S.E. USA

This large deciduous shrub or small tree, up to 20ft (6m) in height, is primarily grown for its superb autumn foliage which turns to shades of orange and red. The individual leaves are broad, paddle-shaped and net-veined. Although the flower clusters are not showy, they have an airy grace. They appear in late spring, remaining until late summer. American smoke tree appreciates a moist acid or neutral soil. It is hardy within the temperate zone, but is best sheltered from strong winds to preserve the autumn colour. It does well in light woodland.

Betula pendula 'Youngii' (Young's weeping birch)

Betulaceae (birch and alder family)

This attractive umbrella-shaped tree is a dwarf weeping form of the common silver birch which rarely exceeds 10ft (3m) in height. The slender hanging stems bear oval to triangular deciduous leaves which take on yellow shades in autumn. The flowers are in the form of yellow catkins which appear in spring while the leaves are still barely emerging from the buds. This birch is totally hardy in the temperate zone and tolerates most soils, including chalky ones providing some humus is worked in at planting time. A stake support will be needed for newly planted trees.

Magnolia X soulangiana

Magnoliacea (magnolia family)

A superb deciduous large shrub or small tree capable of attaining 15ft (4.5m) in height and width, but is usually less. *M. X soulangiana* has large tulip or goblet-shaped white and purple flowers which are borne on naked branches. 'Alba Superba' has large fragrant pure white flowers on an erect vigorous bush; 'Lennei' has enormous goblets stained rose-purple; and 'Rustica Rubra' has rich rosy red-purple cup-shaped blooms. All the forms of *X soulangiana* are hardy in the temperate zone and tolerate a wide range of soil types from acid to alkaline, providing they do not dry out rapidly and contain plenty of humus.

Laburnum anagyroides (golden chain)

Leguminosae (pea family) Europe

A familiar deciduous small tree which can also be grown as a large shrub, attaining 15 to 20ft (4.5 to 6m) in height. The bright green leaves, that deepen with age, are composed of three oval leaflets. In spring, while the leaves are young and silky, bright yellow pea-shaped flowers appear in pendulous chain-like clusters. The small bean-shaped pods which follow are poisonous and should be removed from the reach of young children. *Laburnum* is hardy in all parts of the temperate zone and is tolerant of a wide range of soil types, except those which are very wet.

Malus X purpurea (purple crab-apple)

Rosaceae (rose family) garden hybrid

In gardens, this attractive and familiar crab apple is usually seen as a small tree with a clean trunk. It can be grown as a large bush and kept to 10ft (3m) in height by annual pruning in autumn or winter. The deciduous leaves that are a bright red-purple when young, slowly change to a deeper green-purple. In spring, clusters of rosy-crimson apple flowers appear in profusion. Dark, shiny, red-purple crab-apples mature in late summer to early autumn. Any fertile soil is suitable for this tree and it is hardy in the temperate zone. It makes an eye-catching specimen tree for the smaller lawn.

Cornus kousa chinensis

Magnolia X soulangiana

Cotinus americanus (syn. Rhus cotinoid)

Laburnum anagyroides

Betula pendula 'Youngii'

Malus X purpurea

dwarf shrubs

Not all gardens are large enough to cope with even average-sized shrubs of say 5 to 6ft (1.5 to 1.8m) tall. There may also be areas where tall plants would be out of proportion — on a rock garden or in a small bed or border. Fortunately there are many really small shrubs for just these positions. There are dwarfs with evergreen and deciduous leaves, winter flowering dwarfs, dwarf hedgings and, most noteworthy of all, ground-covers. This is where the dwarf conifers come into their own, as very few gardens have room for the typical pines and firs which look so grand in the large landscape garden.

Shrubs

Berberis stenophylla 'Corallina Compacta'
Ceanothus pumilus
Cotoneaster microphyllus thymifolius
Cytisus X beanii or X kewensis
C. procumbens
Daphne blagayana
D. cneorum
D. collina
D. retusa
Fuchsia 'Tom Thumb'
Halimiocistus sahucii
Helichrysum selago 'Major'
H. pimeleoides 'Glaucocaerulea'
H. albicans
Hypericum moserianum 'Tricolor'
Potentilla fruticosa mandshurica
P. f. 'Munstead Dwarf'
Prunus prostrata
Dwarf Rhododendrons, particularly:-
    impeditum, calostrotum, campylogynum,
    racemosum 'Forrest's Dwarf', 'Carmen',
    'Chink', 'Jenny' ('Creeping Jenny'), 'Blue
    Tit'

Dwarf Conifers

Abies balsamea 'Hudsonia'
Cedrus libani 'Comte de Dijon'
Chamaecyparis lawsoniana 'Pygmaea Argentea',
    C. l. 'Rogersii', 'Minima Glauca'
C. obtusa 'Nana'
C. pisifera 'Boulevard'
Cyptomeria japonica 'Nana' ('Bandi-sugi')
C. j. 'Vilmoriniana'
Juniperus communis 'Compressa'
J. chinensis procumbens
J. horizontalis 'Bar Harbor'
Picea mariana 'Nana'
P. pungens 'Procumbens'
Pinus pumila
P. mugo 'Pumilio'
Podocarpus nivalis
Thuya plicata 'Rogersii'

Thuja orientalis 'Aurea Nana'

Cupressaceae (cypress family)
The bright yellow-green foliage of this evergreen conifer is particularly effective in the winter and associates well with winter-flowering ericas. It forms a dense rounded bush up to 3ft (91cm) composed of erect, flattened frond-like branchlets. The tiny leaves are scale-like and pressed closely to the strongly flattened twigs. This dwarf yellow-foliaged form of the Chinese arbor-vitae very occasionally produces small ovoid cones with horned scales. It will grow in any good garden soil and is hardy in the temperate zone, though severe freezing winds may sear the young foliage.

Fuchsia 'Tom Thumb'

Onagraceae (evening primrose family) garden origin
Raised in France in 1850, this hardy deciduous little fuchsia is still popular. It is the only fuchsia of garden origin that is truly dwarf, rarely 1ft (30cm) tall when grown outside. This tiny fuchsia is erect and bushy and bears pendulous mauve-purple bell-shaped flowers with narrow flared carmine sepals. The flowering season extends from early summer to autumn. Any good garden soil is suitable and a sunny site necessary. Providing the plant is protected with a mound of sand or peat in autumn, it is hardy in all but the coldest parts of the temperate zone.

Juniperus sabina tamariscifolia

Cupressaceae (cypress family) S. Europe
This prostrate mountain form of savin is very popular in temperate countries as ground-cover for banks, as a feature in the larger rock garden or for covering unsightly objects such as drain covers. It forms an evergreen flat-topped shrub with horizontal branches that rarely exceed 2ft (61cm) tall and are often quite prostrate. The leaves are awl-shaped and massed together on the shoots to form plumey branchlets. Blue-black, berry-like cones are sometimes produced on large specimens. Any well-drained soil is suitable and a sunny site gives the most compact growth. It is hardy in the temperate zone.

Chamaecyparis lawsoniana 'Minima'
(miniature Lawson cypress)

Cupressaceae (cypress family)
This small evergreen form of the familiar Lawson cypress is slow-growing, but can eventually attain 6ft (1.8m) in height. This will take 20 years or more, so it can be planted on the smaller rock garden. Once established, it is hardy in the temperate zone, surviving -10°F (-23°C). Any good garden soil is suitable and a sunny site assures compact growth. There are two coloured foliage forms of this miniature Lawson cypress: 'Minima Aurea' has soft golden-green foliage and a conical habit, while 'Minima Glauca' is globular with blue-green leaves.

Picea mariana 'Nana'
(dwarf black spruce)

Pinaceae (pine family) North America
This is the smallest form of the evergreen black spruce and is very slow-growing. Many years elapse before it attains 1ft (30cm) in height. It forms a round dense bushlet; the crowded twigs bear short slender grey-green needle-like leaves. This little conifer is ideal for the smaller rock garden and makes an interesting pot plant for the Alpine house. Any good garden soil is suitable and it is hardy in the temperate zone. Another compact form of *Picea mariana* is 'Doumetii', with a broadly conical outline and an eventual height of 10ft (3m) or so.

Berberis thunbergii 'Atropurpurea Nana'

Berberidaceae (barberry family) Japan
Usually under 2ft (61cm) in height, this dwarf purple-leaved form of *Berberis thunbergii* is ideal as a small dividing hedge or a specimen plant on the larger rock garden. Round-ended leaves are borne in rosette-like clusters along the twigs and are a bright red-purple when young, maturing into a deep green-purple. In autumn they turn red before they fall. Small, pendulous, bowl-shaped yellow flowers open in spring, followed by oval, bead-like red berries. Any ordinary garden soil and a site in sun are all that is necessary. It is hardy in the temperate zone.

Thuja orientalis 'Aurea Nana'

Chamaecyparis lawsoniana 'Minima'

Fuchsia 'Tom Thumb'

Picea mariana 'Nana'

Juniperus sabina tamariscifolia

Berberis thunbergii 'Atropurpurea Nana'

87

ground-cover shrubs

In the temperate zone, any area of bare soil is soon colonized by plants. These colonizers are usually undesirable plants we call weeds. It has become popular to fill in the bare places with desirable plants which compete successfully with the weeds. To be efficient weed smotherers, ground-cover plants must be vigorous and of spreading growth.They should be planted fairly close together to form uninterrupted cover within 2 years.

For shade
Shrubs
Cotoneaster adpressus, C. dammeri, C. horizontalis saxatilis, C. salicifolius 'Repens'
Gaulnettya X wisleyensis
Hedera canariensis 'Variegata'
H. helix 'Hibernica'
Hypericum calycinum
Mahonia aquifolium
Conifers
Cephalotaxus fortunei 'Prostrata'
Taxus baccata 'Repandens', T. b. 'Repens Aurea'

For sun or semi-shade
Shrubs
Arctostaphylos uva-ursi
Berberis candidula, B. verruculosa
Calluna vulgaris (ling) and most cultivars
Cytisus scoparius maritimus ('Prostratus')
Erica (heathers) all hardy species
Hebe 'Carl Teschner', H. pinguifolia 'Pagei', H. rakaiensis (subalpina)
Salix repens 'Argentea'
Conifers
Juniperus communis 'Effusa', J. c. 'Hornibrookii', J. horizontalis, J. conferta, J. sabina 'Tamariscifolia'
Podocarpus alpinus

Steep unmowable slopes
Shrubs
Cotoneaster adpressus 'Praecox', C. horizontalis, C. microphyllus, C. conspicuus 'Decorus', C. c. 'Highlight'
C. salicifolius 'Autumn Fire', C. s. 'Repens'
Genista hispanica
Hypericum calycinum
Potentilla fruticosa 'Longacre', P. f. 'Primrose Beauty', P. f. 'Tangerine', P. 'Elizabeth'
Prunus laurocerasus 'Otto Luyken', P. l. 'Shipkaensis', P. l. 'Zabeliana'
Vinca major

Cytisus X beanii (Bean's broom)

Leguminosae (pea family) garden hybrid
This superb dwarf broom rarely grows much more than 1ft (30cm) tall with stems forming wide arching hummocks. Like most brooms, the small oval leaves do not last long; it is the green stems that provide the framework of the shrub. In late spring these are wreathed in an eye-catching multitude of small golden yellow pea-flowers. This little broom needs a sunny spot and thrives in a wide range of soils, provided they are well-drained. It is hardy in the temperate zone but may be harmed in the coldest regions where prolonged spells of more than 20°F (-11°C) of frost are experienced.

Cotoneaster microphyllus cochleatus

Rosaceae (rose family) China and Tibet
The original wild type of *Cotoneaster microphyllus* is a low-growing, arching-stemmed plant with glossy dark-green foliage and is useful as ground-cover. *C.m. cochleatus* is prostrate, forming wide mats that rise to no more than 3 to 4in (7.6 to 10cm). The tiny evergreen leaves are oval and less glossy. Borne among the leaves during late spring and early summer are small white flowers which give way to pea-sized crimson berries that last all winter, birds permitting. Totally hardy in all parts of the temperate zone, this species will thrive in a wide range of soils, from acid to alkaline, providing they are well-drained.

Calluna vulgaris 'Elsie Purnell'

Ericaceae (heather family) garden origin
Among the evergreen garden heathers the few with double blooms are particularly valuable. Their flowers are bigger and longer lasting than the single-bloomed sorts. 'H. E. Beale' with its bright pink double flowers is the most well known, and its mutant 'Elsie Purnell' has pale silvery pink blooms which open a week or two later in early autumn. Plants can reach 2ft (61cm) or more in height, with an equal spread. All true heathers need a well-drained acid soil, preferably enriched with peat. Although hardy in the temperate zone, long periods of 12°F (-11°C) may damage or kill.

Vinca minor (lesser periwinkle)

Apocynaceae (oleander family) Europe, W. Asia
Tolerant of shade and vigorous, this well-known evergreen is an excellent ground cover. The large blue or purple flowers are borne mainly in spring and summer, with a scattered display well into autumn. Several forms are known, some with variegated foliage, others with blooms that range from white through shades of red-purple to purple-blue. A few have double flowers, the best being 'Azurea Flore Pleno' (blue) and 'Multiplex' (plum-purple). *Vinca minor* is hardy in the temperate zone and thrives in any ordinary garden soil.

Erica cinerea 'Astrosanguinea' (bell heather)

Ericaceae (heather family) W. Europe
Of spreading habit and seldom exceeding 9 to 12in (22.9 to 23cm) tall, the evergreen bell heathers are excellent ground-cover for a sunny site on acid soil. Well branched and slender wiry twigs clad in small, needle-like, dark green leaves form a green carpet pleasing at all times of the year. Some forms have leaves which turn yellow or bronze and coppery-red in winter. Their main period of beauty is from mid-summer to mid-autumn when abundant spikes of rose-purple flowers open. They are hardy in the temperate zone but may suffer damage if temperatures drop to 0°F (-18°C).

Hebe pinguifolia 'Pagei'

Scrophulariaceae (snapdragon family)
Sometimes listed as *Hebe pageana* or *H. pagei*, this evergreen mat-forming shrublet is probably of hybrid origin. It forms mats of bright, bluish-grey leaves in short ascending stems that rarely top 4in (10.2cm). During the spring and early summer a profusion of small glistening white flowers open, often with a scattered display later in the year. Although one of the hardiest of hebes, 'Pagei' is likely to be killed in the coldest parts of the temperate zone where there are long periods of more than 15° to 20°F (-8° to -11°C) of frost. It thrives in any good garden soil that is well-drained but moisture-retentive.

Cytisus X beanii

Vinca minor

Cotoneaster microphyllus cochleatus

Erica cinerea 'Atrosanguinea'

Calluna vulgaris 'Elsie Purnell'

Hebe pinguifolia 'Pagei'

89

exposed sites

There are many sites both inland and by the sea where the winds are strong and frequent and make the growing of plants difficult. One solution is to erect a fence or wall as a barrier or to plant a windbreak of trees or shrubs. The other is to grow only those plants that are known to tolerate or thrive in windy sites. Gardening by the sea has the additional hazard of salt spray drifting inland, especially during gales. If this happens in summer, tender leaves can become scorched and unsightly. Once again there are plants adapted to the seaside environment and among them, several attractive and useful shrubs.

Shrubs

Calluna vulgaris and cultivars (acid soil)
Cistus species
Cornus alba and cultivars
C. Stolonifera 'Flaviramea'
Cotinus coggygria
Cytisus scoparius
Elaeagnus X ebbingei
Escallonia macrantha
Genista hispanica
Halimium ocymoides
Hebe — most species and hybrids
Helianthemum — all species
Hippophae rhamnoides
Hydrangea macrophylla Hortensia and Lacecap
Ilex aquifolium and cultivars
Lavandula species
Olearia X haastii, O. nummularifolia, O. macrodonta
Osmarea burkwoodii
Philadelphus—most species and hybrids
Phillyrea decora
Pittosporum tenuifolium, P. crassifolium
Prunus spinosa 'Purpurea'
Rosa species and cultivars
Santolina species
Senecio greyi
Spartium junceum
Tamarix, all species

Conifers

Cupressus macrocarpa, C. glabra 'Pyramidalis'
Juniperus communis, J. c. 'Hibernica', J. X media 'Pfitzerana', J. chinensis, J. horizontalis
Pinus contorta, P. mugo, P. nigra, P. n. 'Maritima', P. pinaster, P. radiata, P. sylvestris
Taxus baccata

Cordyline australis (cabbage tree)

Liliaceae (Lily family) New Zealand
In the milder parts of the temperate zone this striking small evergreen tree is a good substitute for a palm. Prolonged spells of less than 10° to 15°F (-12° to -9°C) are usually fatal. It can grow to 20ft (6m) but is usually less than half this height. The stem is little-branched, each branch bearing at its tip a tuft of 2ft (61cm) long broad grassy leaves. In summer, mature specimens bear large, open clusters of creamy white flowers, sometimes followed by berries. It will grow in any well-drained soil and beside the sea where salt spray is frequent. Young plants make pleasing specimens in summer bedding schemes.

Escallonia rubra

Escalloniaceae (escallonia family) Chile
Bushy, somewhat rounded growth and arching branches typify this handsome 5 or 6ft (1.5 to 1.8m) tall evergreen shrub. The leaves have a pleasing aromatic fragrance when bruised. They form a fitting background to the clusters of tubular red flowers which are borne in summer. This Chilean shrub will grow in most well-drained soils, though it does not thrive in very dry or chalky ones unless peat or leaf-mould are added. It is not realiably hardy in the temperate zone, being defoliated by freezing winds and cut to ground level by temperatures of 12°F (-11°C).

Olearia X haastii (Haast daisy bush)

Compositae (daisy family) New Zealand
Compact and rounded, this evergreen daisy bush can attain 6ft (1.8m) and more, but is fairly slow-growing and easily kept to 4ft (1.2m) by spring pruning. The oval, thick-textured leaves are small and white-felted beneath. In late summer, every shoot tip is crowded with clusters of small white daisies. Haast daisy bush will grow in any well-drained soil. It is hardy in much of the temperate zone but will not stand temperatures below 0°F (-18°C) and suffers damage from prolonged frosty spells at 10°F (-12°C). Many authorities treat this *olearia* as a species, but is now known to be a hybrid.

Ulex europaeus (common gorse)

Leguminosae (pea family) Europe
Common gorse is a familiar sight on hills and on heathlands. It is a bushy green-stemmed shrub up to 4ft (1.2m) tall. The tiny green leaves last for a few weeks only leaving the green stems. The short lateral twigs are sharply spine-tipped, so this shrub makes a good barrier hedge. From early to mid-spring the stems are smothered with fragrant, bright golden-yellow pea-flowers. A double-flowered form 'Plenus' is an even better garden plant. Gorse will grow in any well-drained soil and is hardy in the temperate zone, though temperatures below 0°F (-18°C) will sear and sometimes kill it.

Philadelphus coronarius (mock orange)

Philadelphaceae (mock orange family) S. E. Europe
Classification of garden forms of mock orange is difficult, as there are several species and many hybrids. The illustration here may be a hybrid. It is, however, typical of the best kind of *philadelphus*, often known as 'syringa'. It is a vigorous deciduous bush up to 10ft (3m) tall with lateral branches arching outwards. In mid-summer an abundance of rich, cup-shaped creamy white flowers are borne which scent the air for yards around. This shrub will grow in any garden soil providing it is not waterlogged. It is hardy in the temperate zone.

Pinus mugo pumilio (dwarf mountain pine)

Pinaceae (pine family) C. Europe
An evergreen capable of reaching 6ft (1.8m) and more, the dwarf mountain pine is often semi-prostrate and ideal for steep rocky exposed places by the sea and inland. The needle-like leaves crowd along the shoots in pairs, and mature specimens bear small woody, pear-shaped cones in late summer. Any well-drained garden soil will suite this low-growing pine. It is totally hardy in the temperate zone. Some authorities classify it as a species, *P. pumilio*: others consider it to be a hybrid with the allied *P. uncinata*, a native of C. and W. European mountains.

Cordyline australis

Ulex europaeus

Escallonia rubra

Philadelphus coronarius

Olearia X haastii

Pinus mugo pumilio

91

hedges & screens

A hedge may serve three main functions: as a dividing barrier, to provide privacy, or as a windbreak. It can range in height from a foot or so, up to 20ft (6m) or more; at Meikleour in Perthshire, Scotland, there is a celebrated beech hedge more than 100ft (30.5m) tall. Hedges above 10ft (3m) in height are often called screens, and it is difficult to define between a hedge and screen when they are large. In general, screens are not clipped, whereas hedges invariably are, if only once a year. Hedges may be of close formal outline and regularly clipped or they may be informal and pruned rather than clipped. The latter are usually flowering hedges, combining utility with beauty.

Hedges 6 to 8ft (1.8 to 2.4m)

(E=evergreen; C=stands clipping)
Berberis x stenophylla (E)
B. thunbergii
B. t. 'Atropurpurea'
Buxus sempervirens (Box) 'Handsworth' (E, C)
Carpinus betulus (Hornbeam) (C)
Cotoneaster franchetii (E)
C. lacteus (E)
Escallonia macrantha and others (E, C)
Euonymus japonicus (E)
Fagus sylvatica(Purple and Green Beech)(C)
Erica mediterranea
E. terminalis (stricta)
E. arborea 'Alpina'
Lavandula spica, particularly:-
L. 'Hidcote' (dwarf hedge) (E, C)
Ilex aquifolium (Common Holly) in variety (E, C)
Ligustrum ovalifolium (Oval-leaved Privet) (E, C)
L. O. 'Aureum' (Gold Privet) (C)
Prunus cistena
Pyracantha—red and yellow berries in variety (E, C)
Potentilla(C)—Many cultivars for low hedges, in particular :-
P. arbuscula 'Elizabeth'
P. fruticosa 'Katherine Dykes'
P. f. 'Friedrichsenii'
P. f. 'Vilminiana'
Rhododendron praecox (E)
Roses in variety, particularly:-
Hybrid Musk 'Penelope'
H. m. 'Buff Beauty'
H. m. 'Wilhelm'
H. m. 'Danae'
H. m. 'Cornelia'
Rosa rugosa 'Rubra'
R. r. 'Frau Dagmar Hastrop'

Taxus baccata 'Fastigiata' (Irish yew)

Taxaceae (yew tree family) Europe to W. Asia
This form of the familiar yew tree grows into a broadly columnar tree of 15ft (4.5m) or more. The dense foliage is composed of dark evergreen, slenderly oblong leaves that end in a short point. Insignificant tiny yellow-green flowers are borne in March and may develop into cup-shaped fruits, pale red and mucilaginous with a polished round nutlet in the centre. Most Irish yews are female only, so unless the rare male of this or the common yew is present, there will be no fruits. Yew thrives in sun or shade and in any well-drained soil. It is hardy in the temperate zone.

Carpinus betulus (common hornbeam)

Carpinaceae (hornbeam family) Europe, Asia Minor
Hornbeam can attain large tree size but responds well to clipping and forms a dense hedge. The dead leaves of autumn hang all winter, keeping it fairly wind-proof and decorative. Yellowish male and green female catkins appear in spring. In late summer curious small ribbed nutlets with a three-lobed wing mature. There are several distinctive forms, noteworthy being 'Fastigiata' ('Pyramidalis'), which is narrowly pyramidal and ideal for a tall screen that does not require clipping. Any fertile soil is suitable and it is hardy in the temperate zone.

Thuja plicata (western red cedar)

Cupressaceae (cypress family) W. North America
This imposing evergreen tree is frequently listed as *Thuja lobbii*. It can be kept to 6ft (1.8m) as a clipped hedge or as an informal screen up to 40ft (12m). Grown untrimmed it can easily grow to 100ft (30m). The tiny scale leaves are bright, almost yellow-green in summer, taking on bronze hues in winter. Ovoid yellow-brown cones, about ½in (1.5cm) long, appear on mature trees in the summer and autumn. The leaves have a pleasant sweetly aromatic odour when crushed. It grows in any ordinary soil that does not dry out and is hardy in the temperate zone.

Fagus sylvatica purpurea (purple beech)

Fagaceae (oak and beech family)
This form of beech can grow into a tree of 60ft (18m) but is easily kept down to 6ft (1.8m) or so by annual pruning in late summer. It makes an excellent dense hedge, retaining the dead russet leaves all winter. Red-purple leaves appear in spring which deepen in colour as they age. *F.s. purpurea* covers varying shades from coppery-red to nearly black-purple, the paler shades being known as copper beech. Any soil is suitable, even thin dry chalky ones, providing they are not waterlogged. It is hardy in the temperate zone. Although tolerant of shade, the best and densest hedges are formed in sunny sites.

Berberis X stenophylla

Berberidaceae (barberry family) garden hybrid
Two South American evergreen barberries *B. darwinii* and *B. empetrifolia* are combined in this highly decorative shrub. *B. X stenophylla* has the height and vigour of *darwinii* and the arching habit and almost needle-like leaves of *empetrifolia*. In spring it is smothered in clusters of small bright orange-yellow flowers. Pruned annually after blooming, it makes an eye-catching informal hedge. Harder, more regular pruning will result in poor flowering. Any fertile soil is suitable if well-drained. It is hardy in all but the coldest parts of the temperate zone.

Prunus cerasifera 'Pissardii' (purple-leaved cherry plum)

Rosaceae (rose family) W. Asia, Balkans and Caucasus
While usually seen as a small standard tree the deciduous purple-leaved cherry plum can be grown as a large bush for screening or as a clipped hedge up to 6ft (1.8m) or so. The oval leaves are bright red-purple when young, but mature to a darker purple in summer. In early spring, before the leaves expand, palest purple plum blossoms open. They are later followed by rounded, reddish plums. It will grow in any ordinary soil that is not waterlogged and is hardy in the temperate zone.

Taxus baccata 'Fastigiata'

Fagus sylvatica purpurea

Carpinus betulus

Berberis X stenophylla

Thuja plicata

Prunus cerasifera 'Pissardii'

93

(hedges cont)
R. r. 'Blanc Double de Coubert'
Rosmarinus officinalis 'Severn Sea' (E, C)
Taxus (Yew) baccata (E, C)

Tall screens

(E=evergreen; C=stands clipping)
Acer campestre (Field Maple) (E)
Chamaecyparis lawsoniana (C), particularly :-
C. l. 'Green Hedger' (E)
Cotoneaster x watereri 'Cornubia' (E)
C. 'Rothschildianus' (E)
X Cupressocyparis leylandii (E, C)
Fagus sylvatica (Purple and Green Beech) (C)
Griselina littoralis
Eucalyptus gunnii and other species (mild
 climates) (C)
Ilex X altaclarensis (Broad-leaved Holly) (C)
Pittosporum tenuifolium and crassifolium (C)
Prunus cerasifera 'Pissardii' (purple-leaved
 Cherry Plum) (C)
P. laurocerasus (Common or Cherry Laurel) (C)
P. lusitanica (Portugese Laurel) (C)
P. spinosa (Blackthorn) (C)
Rhododendron ponticum (C)
R. catawbiense
R. maximum
R. 'Cunningham's White'
R. (and many other hardy hybrids)
Rosa multiflora
Tamarix, all species (C)
Thuya plicata (C)
T. p. 'Fastigiata' ('Stricta')
T. occidentalis

Tamarix gallica (tamarisk)

Tamaricaceae (tamarisk family) S.W. Europe

Frequently grown as a hedge or informal barrier close to the sea, tamarisk is a familiar sight in maritime areas. It can also be grown inland, particularly on windy hillsides or other exposed places. The tiny deciduous leaves are arranged in graceful sprays. In summer they are garlanded with numerous tiny pink flowers which give the appearance of candy floss. Unpruned, tamarisk can attain 10ft (3m), but is easily kept in bounds by annual pruning in winter. It will grow in any soil but needs a sunny site to excell. It is hardy in the temperate zone.

Prunus laurocerasus (cherry laurel)

Rosaceae (rose family) E. Europe, Asia Minor

This common laurel provides a hardy evergreen screen. The glossy bright-green leaves are narrowly oval and often over 6in (15cm) long. Erect spikes of creamy-white flowers appear in late spring. Later small bitter cherries ripen from green to red to black. A well-grown bush can attain 15 to 20ft (4.5 to 6m) in height, but can be kept to a third of this size by spring or autumn pruning. Any well-drained soil is suitable, but peat, leaf-mould or compost should be applied to thin, chalky or sandy soils. It is hardy in the temperate zone and grows in sun or shade.

Chamaecyparis lawsoniana (Lawson cypress or Port Orford cedar)

Cupressaceae (cypress family) N.W. USA

Lawson cypress responds well to clipping and makes a good hedge from 6ft (1.8m) upwards. It can also be used as a screen. When growing naturally it forms a columnar evergreen tree of striking appearance. The leaves are usually a shade of grey or blue-green, but there are other varieties with leaf sprays splashed or suffused with white, cream, yellow or gold. There are also dwarf and miniature forms. During the summer tiny woody cones appear which remain until spring. It is hardy in the temperate zone and will grow in any fertile soil that does not dry out.

Cotoneaster X watereri 'Cornubia'

Rosaceae (rose family) garden hybrid

The Watereri cotoneasters are vigorous, semi-evergreens that can attain a height of 10ft (3m) in fertile soil. 'Cornubia' has glossy oval leaves on stems that arch outwards on mature bushes. In late spring clusters of small creamy flowers appear, followed by abundant red pea-sized fruits. The stems are often pendulous, from the weight of the fruits, and a large specimen bush can be a spectacular sight in autumn and early winter. If the birds are kept away, the berries will last until spring. It is hardy in the temperate zone and will grow in any ordinary soil. A sunny site is best.

Robinia hispida (rose acacia)

Leguminosae (pea family) S.E. USA

In sunny parts of the temperate zone this 8ft (2.5m) tall deciduous shrub makes a beautiful screen. The light, graceful leaves are composed of between 9 and 13 elliptical leaflets. Large, deep pink, pea-shaped blossoms appear in late spring and early summer, borne in loose, pendulous clusters. In winter, the prominent bristly shoots present an interesting silhouette. Any fertile well-drained soil is suitable, but the site must be sunny for a good crop of flowers. It is hardy in the temperate zone, though shoot tips may be damaged in severe winters.

Prunus lusitanica (Portugal laurel)

Rosaceae (rose family) Spain and Portugal

Large, glossy oval deep-green leaves with a reddish stalk typify this handsome evergreen. Unchecked, it will form a broad cone-shaped tree up to 20ft (6m) or more, but if pruned can be kept to 6 or 7ft (1.8 to 2m). It stands moderate exposure to cold winds and will grow in sun or shade and any fertile soil. In thin chalky soils add some well-rotted manure, peat or compost. It is hardy in much of the temperate zone but can be damaged by temperatures below 0°F (-18°C). In summer, slender spikes of small white scented flowers appear, followed by bitter black-purple cherries.

Tamarix gallica

Cotoneaster X watereri 'Cornubia'

Prunus laurocerasus

Robinia hispida

Chamaecyparis lawsoniana

Prunus lusitanica

95

planning a small town garden

Many town gardens are nothing more than a square or rectangular patch between two rows of back-to-back terrace houses, often not more than 15ft (4.5m) square. If left completely alone such a back yard can be an eyesore—especially when seen through a sitting room or dining room window.

A tiny garden is almost always enclosed and one or two of its walls may be formed by the back or sides of another house. This enclosure is often an advantage: high walls shut off noise, besides giving privacy, plus a lot more gardening space. But as the brickwork will be seen when the last leaves have fallen from the covering creepers, it is important that the walls are considered as an integral part of the garden itself.

These mini-gardens need treating in quite a different way from larger ones. The central area is best left open, either paved or with a lawn, with planting concentrated round the outer edge of the garden. Note the use of large, bold shrubs round the wall—a scaled-down version of the conventional herbaceous border planted down one side would not only look dull but cramped as well.

The area has been made more interesting with the use of different levels and terracing against the walls. Paving is used to keep the front area neat. The final result is a charming, private walled garden, ideal for sitting in on sunny days.